Love and Hate for God's Sake

Written by Mujtaba Sabouri

Translated by Saleem Bhimji

Edited by Arifa Hudda

ISBN: 978-1-927930-44-1

Love And Hate for God's Sake

Written by Mujtaba Sabouri
Translated by Saleem Bhimji
Edited by Arifa Hudda

Cover Design and Layout by Islamic Publishing House (www.iph.ca)

Contents

Foreword by the Translator....i

Summary of the Discussion....vii

Introduction to the Topic....9
Meanings of Sabb and Laʿn....10
Malediction in the Quran....13
  Examples of Malediction in the Quran....13
  Quran and Malediction Upon Individuals....17
Prophet Muḥammad ﷺ and Malediction....18
The Companions and Malediction....20
The Ahl as-Sunnah and Malediction....22
The Wisdom Behind Malediction....25
Malediction and Muslim Unity....28
Conclusion....36
The Quran and Malediction....39
  1. Malediction against Satan....39
  2. Malediction against the Disbelievers....40
  2.1 General Verses....40
  2.2 Specific Verses – Those who Left the Faith....41
  2.3 Disbelievers from Amongst the Tribe of ʿĀd....41
  2.4 Disbelievers from Amongst the People of the Pharaoh....41
  2.5 Disbelievers from Amongst the Tribes of Israel....42
  2.6 Disbelievers from Amongst the People of the Book....44
  3. Malediction against the Polytheists....46

4. Malediction against Specific Individuals from among... 46
4.1 Those who Disregarded the Sabbath.......................................46
4.2 Claimants that the hands of Allah ﷻ are "Tied" 47
5. Malediction against Specific Individuals who claimed..........48
5.1 The Hypocrites...48
5.2 The "Cursed Tree" in the Quran..49
6. Malediction against People – Muslims and non-Muslims 51
6.1 Those who Cause Grief to Allah ﷻ and his Messenger ﷺ.51
6.1.1 Hurting Imam ʿAlī ؑ is like hurting the Prophet ﷺ.......51
6.1.2 Hurting Fāṭima az-Zahrāʾ ؑ is like hurting... 53
6.2 Those who Lie 53
6.3 Those who Kill Innocent People..54
6.4 The Oppressors and Despots..54
6.5 Those who Falsely Accuse Women of Adultery....................55
6.6 Those who Break their Oaths Made to Allah ﷻ....................56
6.7 Those who Attribute Falsehood Against Allah ﷻ................56
6.8 Those who Hide the Truths of Allah ﷻ..................................57
6.9 Those who Consider the Jews to be Better than... 57
6.10 Those who Create Corruption on the Earth and... 58

Sources 59

Other Publications Available...61

In the Name of Allah,
the All-Compassionate,
the All-Merciful

Foreword by the Translator

Emotions play a powerful role in the life of the human being.

Many times, people eat based on how they feel – and that is why some over-eat or indulge in harmful foods when they are going through difficult situations in their life.

In addition, emotions also control how we act, interact, and react to people around us. People can be triggered simply by being told something to their face.

Seeing as how emotions play such a role in our lives, it is no surprise that Allah ﷻ has spoken about this natural human process in the Quran and Prophet Muḥammad ﷺ and the Ahlul Bayt ؑ have also highlighted this area in their traditions.

From all the emotions we have, two of most powerful, and without doubt, the most divisive within the Muslim community today is the concept of 'love and hate' as it relates to personalities in the history of Islam.

Once the mission of Prophet Muḥammad ﷺ began in Mecca, he employed many tools to educate the Quraysh and others to the religion of Islam – never practicing "hate". Rather, even when he was pelted with stones, mocked, insulted, and called vicious nicknames, he would constantly pray to Allāh ﷻ saying, "O Allāh, please guide my people as they do not know."[1]

Although Prophet Muḥammad ﷺ never gave up on inviting people to the path of Allāh ﷻ, through revelation, he would be told that some people, such as Abū Lahab and is wife Umm Jamīlah would never accept Islam. Therefore, when Allāh ﷻ refers to them in the Quran, he does so by saying: "May both hands of Abu Lahab be ruined, and are ruined are they! His wealth has not availed him, nor his gains. He will enter a flaming Fire to roast. And (with him) his wife, carrier of firewood (and of evil tales and slander). Around her neck will be a halter of strongly twisted rope."[2]

With that said, this book, *Love and Hate for God's Sake*, is a review and analysis of verses of the Quran, ḥadīth and historical references in which the concept of malediction (laʿn) is discussed. Far from being profanity or vulgarity, as you will see, the laʿn is nothing more than what we can term a 'negative' supplication. What we mean by this is that if praying for one's wellness, income, strength, etc. are all regarded as 'positive' supplications in which we ask Allāh ﷻ to bestow His special Mercy and Blessings upon someone or a group of people, then laʿn is the opposite: we pray to Allāh ﷻ, sincerely asking Him to remove His special Mercy and Blessings from a particular individual or community.

---

[1] *Al-Kharā'ij wal Jarā'iḥ*, Vol. 1, Pg. 164:

أَللّٰهُمَّ اهْدِ قَوْمِي فَإِنَّهُمْ لَا يَعْلَمُونَ.

[2] Quran, Sūrah al-Lahab (111), Verses 1-5:

تَبَّتْ يَدَآ أَبِي لَهَبٍ وَتَبَّ ۝١ مَآ أَغْنَىٰ عَنْهُ مَالُهُۥ وَمَا كَسَبَ ۝٢ سَيَصْلَىٰ نَارًا ذَاتَ لَهَبٍ ۝٣ وَٱمْرَأَتُهُۥ حَمَّالَةَ ٱلْحَطَبِ ۝٤ فِي جِيدِهَا حَبْلٌ مِّن مَّسَدٍۭ ۝٥

Some may wonder that is it necessary to send laʿn upon someone? If they were bad people, then surely Allāh ﷻ will deal with them with His justice and deprive them of His mercy; just as He will bless and aide those who work in his way – regardless of whether we pray for them and their success.

Although that is a valid point, however at the same time, we have countless traditions as well as verses of the Quran encouraging us to supplicate to Allāh ﷻ for our physical and spiritual needs. In addition, as we will see when reviewing the verses of the Quran, Allāh ﷻ has condoned and even accepted believers making laʿn on certain individuals and groups.

We must also realize that dūʿāʾ - both the 'positive' and 'negative' forms are not just words to say – they are meant to evoke a change in our heart. When someone prays to Allāh ﷻ for a spouse or a better job, they cannot suffice with merely the dūʿāʾ - they need to go out and work at what they are asking Allāh ﷻ for. Allāh ﷻ will hear and accept the supplication, but He will not transport a spouse to the person's doorstep; nor will He fill a person's bank account with money!

Rather, the dūʿāʾ is also evoked to make a change in ourselves. When we pray for extra sustenance, yes we understand that we are asking Allāh ﷻ for this sustenance and for Him to facilitate it for us and to make it easy for us to attain it and also for us not to have unnecessary expenses that deplete our wealth. But then at the same time, we go and work harder and do what we can to increase our sustenance.

Similar is the laʿn. When we ask Allāh ﷻ to deprive certain people or groups of His Mercy and Blessings, we must also know who those people are, study history to see what they did that would warrant such a supplication against them and then resolve in our hearts not to do what they did – lest we imprecate against ourselves and become the cause of our own destruction.

Thus, we must realize that the supplication of laʿn is not just an empty word – it is a carefully thought-out prayer to Allāh ﷻ

in which we also resolve not to do what others have done. It is to ensure that we have reformed ourselves, lest the pray returns to us.

By way of example, if we reflect on the last portion of this verse in which we read: "...and then let us pray and invoke God's curse upon those who lie."[3]

If we are habituated to lying to family, friends, co-workers, customers, etc. and we read this verse on a frequent basis, then it stands to reason that we are actually invoking the curse of Allāh ﷻ against ourselves! Granted that the overall theme of this verse was in regards to the event of the Christians of Najrān coming to Medina to meet and debate with Prophet Muḥammad ﷺ in regard to what they felt was the divine nature of Prophet ʿIsā ؑ, however it can also be understood on its own – as this theme runs through the Quran.

So, we can see that evoking the laʿn is not an easy thing and should not be taken lightly. We need to ensure that when we utter these words against someone or a group of the Muslim community, we do so with full awareness of what we are getting ourselves into. We need to ensure that we are not doing the same crimes they are guilty of, otherwise, as we previously said, we risk running the danger of praying for Allāh ﷻ to remove His Mercy and Blessings from us!

With that said, we conclude this introduction and ask Allāh ﷻ to accept this effort from us to present the beautiful teachings of the Quran. We ask that this book and its contents are understood in the light in which we have intended it to be – and that is not to cause division and strife in the Muslim community, but rather, to uncover one of the lesser-known teachings of the Quran and the

---

[3] Quran. Sūrah Āl ʿImrān (3), Verse 61:

ثُمَّ نَبْتَهِلْ فَنَجْعَل لَّعْنَتَ ٱللَّهِ عَلَى ٱلْكَٰذِبِينَ ﴿٦١﴾

Sunnah of Prophet Muḥammad ﷺ and his immaculate successors – the Ahlul Bayt ﷺ.

We pray to Allāh ﷻ that He accept this act of worship and that he allows the eyes of the Muslim community to be opened to the powerful and practical teachings of the Quran.

ٱلَّذِينَ يُبَلِّغُونَ رِسَٰلَٰتِ ٱللَّهِ وَيَخْشَوْنَهُۥ وَلَا يَخْشَوْنَ أَحَدًا إِلَّا ٱللَّهَ ۗ وَكَفَىٰ بِٱللَّهِ حَسِيبًا ٣٩

"Those who deliver the messages of Allah and fear Him, and do not fear any one but Allah; and Allah is sufficient to take account."

Quran, Sūrah al-Aḥzāb (33), Verse 39

Saleem Bhimji
Director *of* Islamic Publishing House
March 23rd, 2023 CE
Ramaḍān 1st, 1444 AH

Summary of the Discussion

The terms cussing[4] - *"sabb"* (سبّ), swearing[5] - *"shaṭam"* (شطم), and - malediction[6] - *"la'n"* (لعن), in their truest forms, represent the totality of enmity, and the appreciation of these terms and their usage has been present right from the initial stages of human existence and historically speaking, there have been individuals, who in order to show their enmity in regards to events which transpired in the past, or individuals who lived in long-ago times, who have demonstrated these terms vividly in their lives.

Even after the introduction of Islam, the usage and real-world practice of these terms was common and there were some individuals, who to express their aversion and detestation for the acts of others resorted to *cussing* - *"sabb"* (سبّ) and *malediction* - *"la'n"* (لعن). As these practices were commonplace, it is important for us to analyse these terms from an Islamic perspective and to conduct an in-depth investigation into them.

In this book, what we seek to do through our study is to explore the phenomenon of *cussing* and *malediction* and its status

---

[4] Generally, in English, this word is used to mean cursing, cussing, swearing, bad language, foul language, obscenities, expletives, or vulgarism and is considered as socially offensive use of language. (Tr.)

[5] As swearing has multiple meanings – some of which are praiseworthy, we use it in this book to mean 'the use of offensive language, especially as an expression of anger.' (Tr.)

[6] This word can also be interchangeably used with terms such as: imprecation, execration, malison, anathema, or commination and is considered as any expressed with that some form of adversity or misfortune befall or attach to one or more persons, a place, or an object from a supernatural or spiritual power – in the context of our discussion this is from Allah ﷻ. Throughout this book, wherever the original author has used the word *la'n* or one of its derivatives in Farsi, we have translated it as malediction. (Tr.)

from the Islamic point of view by delving into the relevant sources: the Quran, the Prophetic traditions *(aḥādīth)* and the conduct of the Muslims.

In addition, through reviewing the historical evidence and by means of a psychological analysis, we will seek to prove that *cussing* - *"sabb"* (سبّ) and *swearing* - *"shaṭam"* (شطم) are absolutely forbidden *(ḥarām)* in the sacred teachings of Islam; however as for *malediction* - *"laʿn"* (لعن), it is something which is essential from the societal point of view.

We will see how the permissibility of *malediction* - *"laʿn"* (لعن) is something which all the Muslim scholars agree upon and that what we see today from the Wahhabi sect and those who follow this group which has become prevalent in the world in which they categorize *malediction* alongside *cussing* and *swearing* and claim that all of these go against the teachings of Islam, is nothing other than baseless and futile claims which lack any form of evidence.

Introduction to the Topic

The stances of love and hate are two extremely powerful forces within a person which can be a source of great benefit for the society on a whole and an individual on his own, and it is for this reason that Islam has placed a lot of attention on them, such that the Noble Prophet of Islam ﷺ has been quoted as saying:

هَلِ الْإِيمَانُ إِلَّا الْحُبُّ وَالْبُغْضُ

Is true faith anything other than love and hate?[7]

Being endowed with the power of love and adoration and manifesting these traits vis-à-vis the person who is acting with goodness is the actual show of love of a person towards good itself; and this stance towards love is a cherished guide to assist a person in reaching towards perfection and spiritual happiness.

In the same vein, taking a stand and expressing abhorrence and aversion towards individuals who have sunk to the lowest levels of depravity in which they have permitted themselves to commit the most heinous of atrocities and reach the bottom levels of baseness, is, the explicit confirmation of aversion to wickedness itself and keeping away from everything which will distance a person from Allah ﷻ.

The noble companions who lived during the time of Prophet Muḥammad ﷺ, were fully aware of the life of the Noble Messenger ﷺ and in addition, because they possessed a special status, they managed to gain the attention of all the believers – even though all the companions were not at the same spiritual level.

Some of them were not able to remain firm on the path of true faith and some of them even ended up drifting away entirely from the path which they had chosen during the lifetime of the

[7] *Biḥār al-Anwār*, Vol. 66, Pg. 241.

Prophet ﷺ. It is due to this fact that today, it is necessary that those who brought about true faith during the lifetime of the Messenger of Allah ﷺ and remained on the straight path until the end of their lives and the individuals who were led astray while traversing the straight path and performed actions which went against the ways of the Noble Prophet ﷺ and transgressed his commandments – need to be understood and distinguished from one another.

Regarding the first group, we must show love and affection; while regarding the second group and their base actions, we must display our disgust and distance ourselves from their un-ethical deeds.

Therefore, according to the habit of Allah ﷻ in the Quran, the Muslims must invoke the *malediction* of Allah ﷻ and must seek aversion from that group whose atrocities and opposition to the orders and dictates of the Noble Prophet ﷺ reached such a critical level that it resulted in the misguidance of many other individuals.

Meanings of Sabb and Laʿn

There is a difference between *malediction* and *cussing*. In Islam, *cussing* is forbidden *(ḥarām)*; and in the books of lexicon, *"sabb"* is defined as cussing and the usage of profanities.[8]

Al-Zabīdī has stated: "*Al-sabb* is defined as cussing."[9]

Ibne Manḍhūr has stated that: "*Al-Shaṭam* means offensive speech and there is no requirement that in such speech, defamation occurs."[10]

---

[8] *Al-Ṣiḥāḥ fīl Lughah*, Vol. 1, Pg. 299.

[9] *Tāj al-ʿUrūs*, Vol. 2, Pg. 63:

أَلسَّبُ: أَلْشَتَمُ.

[10] *Lisān al-ʿArab*, Vol. 12, Pg. 318:

Al-Ṭurayḥī has stated: "*al-Shaṭam* means to describe something such as to show a deficiency within it."[11]

Islam has prohibited the acts of *cussing* and the use of vulgar language just as Allah ﷻ, has stated:

﴿وَلَا تَسُبُّوا۟ ٱلَّذِينَ يَدْعُونَ مِن دُونِ ٱللَّهِ فَيَسُبُّوا۟ ٱللَّهَ عَدْوًۢا بِغَيْرِ عِلْمٍ...﴾

> Do not cuss those whom they invoke besides Allah, lest they should abuse Allah out of hostility, without any knowledge...[12]

The Noble Prophet of Islam ﷺ was extraordinarily strong in his words in condemning this practice and has stated: "Cussing and usage of vulgar language towards a Muslim is a sin."[13]

During the battle of Ṣiffīn, when the Commander of the Faithful ʿAlī ibn Abī Ṭālib ؑ was informed that some of his companions where using bad language in regards to the people of the Levant *(Shām)*, he addressed them by saying: "I dislike that you start to verbally abuse them (using vulgar language), but if you describe their deeds and recount their situations (their actions) that would be a better mode of speaking and a more convincing way of arguing [with others about how these people are]."[14]

أَلشَّتَمُ: قَبِيحِ الْكَلَامِ وَلَيْسَ فِيهِ قَذفٌ.

[11] *Majmaʿ al-Baḥrayn*, Vol. 12, Pg. 70.

[12] Quran, Sūrah al-Anʿām (6), Verse 108.

[13] *Ṣaḥīḥ al-Bukhārī*, Vol. 1, Pg. 52; Al-Kāfī, Vol. 2, Pg. 360:

سِبَابُ الْمُسْلِمِ فُسُوقٌ

[14] *Nahj al-Balāghah*, Pg. 323:

In addition, Imam Jaʿfar as-Ṣādiq ﵇ has stated: "The cussing of a believer [by another believer] is like the one who has thrown himself into perdition."[15]

Therefore, *cussing* is recognized as something which is expressly forbidden *(ḥarām)* in Islam and any sane and rational person will be sure to refrain from such actions; however as for evoking *malediction*, this is something other than *cussing* and its meaning is to "distance oneself towards something good."

Al-Jawharī has stated: "*Al-Laʿn* is to driveway and to distance oneself away [from evil and going towards] good."[16]

In addition, malediction has also been defined as displaying an aversion towards an individual's despicable actions.

Rāghib al-Iṣfhānī has stated that: "Malediction means the rejection and distancing of oneself from something - angrily. If malediction is practiced by Allah, then its meaning is that in the next life, one will face the Divine retribution; while in the transient world, it means that the individual will be cut off from being able to accept the mercy [of Allah ﷻ] and the Divine providence. If malediction is employed by an individual, then it means that one makes supplication and imprecation and entreats [Allah ﷻ] to bring about damage to the person against whom one is praying."[17]

إِنِّي أَكْرَهُ لَكُمْ أَنْ تَكُونُوا سَبَّابِينَ وَلٰكِنَّكُمْ لَوْ وَصَفْتُمْ أَعْمَالَهُمْ وَذَكَرْتُمْ حَالَهُمْ، كَانَ أَصْوَبَ فِي الْقَوْلِ وَأَبْلَغَ فِي الْعُذْرِ.

15 *Wasāʾil ash-Shīʿa*, Vol. 12, Pg. 298:

سَبَابُ الْمُؤْمِنُ كَالْمُشْرِفِ عَلَى الْهَلَكَةِ.

16 *Ṣiḥāḥ al-Jawharī*, Vol. 6, Pg. 2196; *Lisān al-ʿArab*, Vol. 13, Pg. 387:

أَلْلَعْنُ، الطَرْدُ وَالْإِبْعَادُ مِنَ الْخَيْرِ.

17 *Al-Mufradāt*, Vol. 2, Pg. 339.

Therefore, malediction means to distance oneself from the despicable actions of an individual and to pray that he is detached from the mercy of Allah ﷻ.

The best way to phrase this word is to state that it means: "May Allah never forgive you." For example, in some instances it may be said of an individual: "May Allah never forgive that person whose actions led to the killing of countless innocent people" – this is malediction.

Such phrases can never be positive or in a person's benefit [although one is praying "for" someone else]; rather, the supplication against a person (imprecation) is since one has committed a contemptible action, and therefore when a person says: "O Allah! Remove your mercy from such and such person," what we mean is that we are asking Allah ﷻ to leave that person alone on his own and not forgive him for his evil actions.

Malediction in the Quran

In the Noble Quran, Allah ﷻ has expressed His malediction and His imprecation on various groups of individuals and this is evidence of it being permissible to use this word.

Therefore, although we see that the usage of *cussing* has been prohibited in the Quran, however there are many instances in which *malediction* has been used.

Examples of Malediction in the Quran

By referring to the verses of the Noble Quran, we can deduce that Allah ﷻ has expressed His malediction upon certain individuals and upon certain groups of people – the following are some examples:

1. Satan:

﴿وَإِنَّ عَلَيْكَ لَعْنَتِي إِلَىٰ يَوْمِ ٱلدِّينِ ۝﴾

...and indeed, **My malediction** will be on you (Satan) until the Day of Retribution.[18]

2. Belligerent disbelievers:

﴿إِنَّ ٱللَّهَ لَعَنَ ٱلْكَٰفِرِينَ وَأَعَدَّ لَهُمْ سَعِيرًا ۝﴾

Indeed, Allah has **applied malediction** upon the faithless and prepared for them a blaze...[19]

3. Certain individuals from amongst the Banī Isrāʾīl – the progeny of Prophet Yaʿqūb – those that did not believe in the prophets which Allah sent to them and remained as non-believers:

﴿لُعِنَ ٱلَّذِينَ كَفَرُوا۟ مِنۢ بَنِىٓ إِسْرَٰٓءِيلَ عَلَىٰ لِسَانِ دَاوُۥدَ وَعِيسَى ٱبْنِ مَرْيَمَ ۚ ذَٰلِكَ بِمَا عَصَوا۟ وَّكَانُوا۟ يَعْتَدُونَ ۝﴾

The faithless among the Banī Isrāʾīl **were maledicted** on the tongue of Dāwūd and ʿIsā, son of Maryam. That is because they would disobey [the commandments] and used to commit transgression.[20]

4. Oppressors:

﴿...أَلَا لَعْنَةُ ٱللَّهِ عَلَى ٱلظَّٰلِمِينَ ۝﴾

---

[18] Quran, Sūrah Ṣwād (38), Verse 78.
[19] Ibid., Sūrah al-Aḥzāb (33), Verse 64.
[20] Ibid., Sūrah al-Māʾidah (5), Verse 78.

Look! The **curse** (removal of the mercy) of Allah is upon the wrongdoers.[21]

5. Liars:

﴿وَٱلۡخَٰمِسَةُ أَنَّ لَعۡنَتَ ٱللَّهِ عَلَيۡهِ إِن كَانَ مِنَ ٱلۡكَٰذِبِينَ ٧﴾

...and a fifth [oath] that Allah's **malediction** shall be upon him if he were lying.[22]

6. Those who hurt Prophet Muḥammad ﷺ:

﴿إِنَّ ٱلَّذِينَ يُؤۡذُونَ ٱللَّهَ وَرَسُولَهُۥ لَعَنَهُمُ ٱللَّهُ فِي ٱلدُّنۡيَا وَٱلۡأٓخِرَةِ وَأَعَدَّ لَهُمۡ عَذَابٗا مُّهِينٗا ٥٧﴾

Indeed, those who torment Allah, and His Apostle are **cursed** (removed from mercy) by Allah in the world and in the Hereafter...[23]

7. Those who falsely accuse women of illicit sexual improprieties:

﴿إِنَّ ٱلَّذِينَ يَرۡمُونَ ٱلۡمُحۡصَنَٰتِ ٱلۡغَٰفِلَٰتِ ٱلۡمُؤۡمِنَٰتِ لُعِنُواْ فِي ٱلدُّنۡيَا وَٱلۡأٓخِرَةِ وَلَهُمۡ عَذَابٌ عَظِيمٞ ٢٣﴾

Indeed, those who accuse honourable and unwary faithful women shall be **cursed** in this world and the Hereafter...[24]

---

[21] Quran., Sūrah Hūd (11), Verse 18.
[22] Ibid., Sūrah al-Nūr (24), Verse 7.
[23] Ibid., Sūrah al-Aḥzāb (33), Verse 57.
[24] Ibid., Sūrah al-Nūr (24), Verse 23.

8. Those who kill innocent believers:

﴿وَمَن يَقْتُلْ مُؤْمِنًا مُّتَعَمِّدًا فَجَزَآؤُهُۥ جَهَنَّمُ خَٰلِدًا فِيهَا وَغَضِبَ
ٱللَّهُ عَلَيْهِ وَلَعَنَهُۥ وَأَعَدَّ لَهُۥ عَذَابًا عَظِيمًا ٩٣﴾

Should anyone kill a believer intentionally, his requital shall be hell, to remain in it [forever]; Allah shall be wrathful to him and **maledict against him** and He will prepare for him a great punishment.[25]

9. Hypocrites:

﴿وَعَدَ ٱللَّهُ ٱلْمُنَٰفِقِينَ وَٱلْمُنَٰفِقَٰتِ وَٱلْكُفَّارَ نَارَ جَهَنَّمَ خَٰلِدِينَ فِيهَا ۚ
هِىَ حَسْبُهُمْ ۚ وَلَعَنَهُمُ ٱللَّهُ ۖ وَلَهُمْ عَذَابٌ مُّقِيمٌ ٦٨﴾

Allah has promised the hypocrites, men, and women, and the faithless - the Fire of Hell, to remain in it [forever]. That suffices them. Allah has evoked **malediction upon them**, and there is a lasting punishment for them.[26]

10. Those who spread corruption and sever their family ties:

﴿فَهَلْ عَسَيْتُمْ إِن تَوَلَّيْتُمْ أَن تُفْسِدُوا۟ فِى ٱلْأَرْضِ وَتُقَطِّعُوٓا۟
أَرْحَامَكُمْ ٢٢ أُو۟لَٰٓئِكَ ٱلَّذِينَ لَعَنَهُمُ ٱللَّهُ فَأَصَمَّهُمْ وَأَعْمَىٰٓ
أَبْصَٰرَهُمْ ٢٣﴾

May it not be that if you were to wield authority you would cause corruption in the land and ill-treat your blood relations? They are the ones upon whom Allah has evoked

[25] Quran, Sūrah al-Nisā’ (4), Verse 93.
[26] Ibid., Sūrah al-Tawbah (9), Verse 68.

> **malediction** upon, so He made them deaf, and blinded their sight.[27]

Quran and Malediction Upon Individuals

Just as was previously explained, the Noble Quran has itself imprecated against someone groups of individuals who possessed certain negative traits, and by applying the general imprecations mentioned in these verses into specific historical examples, we see that the words of the Quran fit some of the companions of the Prophet ﷺ; however, in other instances, there are clear verses of specific companions who have been imprecated against. One such verse of the Quran is the following:

﴿وَإِذْ قُلْنَا لَكَ إِنَّ رَبَّكَ أَحَاطَ بِٱلنَّاسِ ۚ وَمَا جَعَلْنَا ٱلرُّءْيَا ٱلَّتِىٓ أَرَيْنَـٰكَ إِلَّا فِتْنَةً لِّلنَّاسِ وَٱلشَّجَرَةَ ٱلْمَلْعُونَةَ فِى ٱلْقُرْءَانِ ۚ وَنُخَوِّفُهُمْ فَمَا يَزِيدُهُمْ إِلَّا طُغْيَـٰنًا كَبِيرًا ﴿٦٠﴾﴾

> When We said to you, 'Indeed your Lord comprehends all humanity,' We did not appoint the vision that We showed you except as a test for the people and the **tree cursed** in the Quran. We deter them, but it only increases them in great rebellion.[28]

In relation to the exegesis of this verse, the commentators of the Noble Quran have stated that the meaning of the "cursed tree" is the family tree and lineage of Ḥakam ibn Abīl ʿĀṣ; and the meaning of the 'vision' which was seen is the dream which the

---

[27] Quran, Sūrah Muḥammad (47), Verse 22-23.
[28] Ibid., Sūrah al-Isrāʾ (17), Verse 60.

Noble Prophet ﷺ saw in which the children of Marwān ibn Ḥakam were one by one, ascending his pulpit *(mimbar)*.[29]

Prophet Muḥammad ﷺ and Malediction

By referring to the *aḥādīth*, we notice that the Noble Prophet ﷺ used the term *laʿn* and its derivatives many times – even using it specifically for some Muslims and even some of the companions - and in all these instances, he did so due to their shameful actions.

Sometimes, the Noble Prophet ﷺ used the term *laʿn* in a general meaning, such as when he stated: "The thief, the young man who comes out looking like a woman and also the woman whose appearance is that of a man, the person who slaughters an animal without taking the name of Allah ﷻ, the person who imprecates against his own parents, the one who engages in the same actions (homosexuality) as the people of Lūṭ and the one who takes bribes [are all those who have been distanced from the mercy of Allah]..."[30]

The Prophet of Islam ﷺ has also been quoted as saying: "May Allah remove His mercy *(laʿn)* from alcoholic drinks, the one who drinks alcohol, the one who serves alcohol, the seller, the purchaser and..."[31]

The Prophet of Islam ﷺ has also said: "May Allah remove His mercy *(laʿn)* from the one who takes usury, the one who gives usury, the one who writes [a contract based on usury] and the witnesses [who witness a transaction involving usury]."[32]

There are times in which the Noble Prophet ﷺ also mentioned specific individuals and made imprecation against them.

---

29 *Tafsīr al-Kabīr*, Vol. 21, Pg. 365.

30 *Musnad Aḥmad ibn Ḥanbal*, Vol. 2, Pg. 152-225.

31 *Sunan* of Abī Dāwūd, Vol. 3, Pg. 366; *Musnad Aḥmad ibn Ḥanbal*, Vol. 1, Pg. 316

32 Ibid., Vol. 1, Pg. 93

Shaʿbī has narrated that: "While leaning against the Kaʿbah, ʿAbdullāh ibn Zubayr stated: 'I take an oath by the Lord of this house that indeed the Messenger of Allah had imprecated against so and so and whosoever was born from his loins."[33] In regards to whom it was that ʿAbdullāh ibn Zubayr was referring to, it has been mentioned by Ḥākim al-Nishābūrī in a tradition found in his *Mustadrak* that the person was Ḥakam ibn ʿĀṣ and his son.[34]

In addition, Marwān and his father were also people who the Messenger of Allah ﷺ imprecated against. Ḥākim al-Nishābūrī has narrated a tradition found in his *Mustadrak* that states: "The Messenger of Allah imprecated against the father of Marwān even before Marwān was born."[35]

On various occasions, the Messenger of Allah ﷺ imprecated against Abū Sufyān and Muʿāwiyah. ʿAlī ibn Aqmar has stated: "Along with a group of others, we asked ʿAbdullāh ibn ʿUmar to share a saying of the Prophet with us to which he replied: 'While Abū Sufyān was on his steed and Muʿāwiyah and his brothers were in front and behind their father (Abū Sufyān) riding on their animals, the Prophet said the following (regarding them): 'O Allah! Remove Your mercy from the one who is riding [on the animal] at the front, the one who is following him and the one who is behind him.' We asked him [ʿAbdullāh ibn ʿUmar]: 'You heard this directly from the Messenger of Allah?' He replied: 'Yes

---

[33] *Musnad Aḥmad ibn Ḥanbal*, Vol. 4, Pg. 5:

لَقَدْ لَعَنَ رَسُولُ اللهِ فُلَانًا وَمَا وُلِدَ مِنْ صُلْبِهِ.

[34] *Mustadrak*, Vol. 4, Pg. 528:

لَعَنَ رَسُولُ اللهِ الحَكَمَ وَوَلَدَهُ.

[35] *Mustadrak*, Vol. 4, Pg. 528:

رَسُولُ اللهِ لَعَنَ أَبَا مَرْوَانَ وَمَرْوَانُ فِي صُلْبِهِ.

and if I lie, may both of my ears go deaf and my I lose my sight.'"[36]

In another event, ʿAbdullāh ibn ʿUmar said: "The Messenger of Allah ﷺ once imprecated in the following fashion during the Battle of Uḥud by saying: 'O Allah! Remove Your mercy from Abū Sufyān...'[37]

In addition, Ibn Barrāʾ has narrated from his father, Barrāʾ ibn ʿĀzib that Abū Sufyān, along with his son Muʿāwiyah, came to the Messenger ﷺ, who said to them: "O Allah! Remove your mercy from the one who is following [Muʿāwiyah] and the one whom he is following [Abū Sufyān]. O Allah! I leave '*al-Aqyas*' to you [to deal with].' Ibne Barrā' asked his father, "Who is *al-Aqyas*?" The father replied, "This is Muʿāwiyah."[38]

The Companions and Malediction

Through a historical analysis, we conclude that there were some companions of Prophet Muḥammad ﷺ who engaged in the act of invoking malediction against other companions.

In a letter which he wrote to Muʿāwiyah, Muḥammad ibn Abī Bakr (the son of Abū Bakr) mentioned that he (Muʿāwiyah) and his father were both individuals who were imprecated against

[36] *Waqaʿat al-Ṣiffīn*, Pg. 217:

أَللَّهُمَّ الْعَنِ الْقَائِدَ وَالسَّائِقَ وَالرَّاكِبَ، قُلْنَا أَنْتَ سَمِعْتَ رَسُولَ اللهِ (صَلَّى اللّهُ عَلَيْهِ وَآلِهِ)؟ قَالَ: نَعَمْ، وَإِلَّا فُصِمْتَا أُذُنَایَ، كَمَا عُمِيتَا عَيْنَایَ.

[37] *Tafsīr of al-Ṭabarī*, Vol. 7, Pg. 200:

أَللّٰهُمَّ الْعَنْ أَبَا سُفْيانَ...

[38] *Al-Ghadīr*, Vol. 12, Pg. 140; *Waqaʿat al-Ṣiffīn*, Pg. 218:

أَللّٰهُمَّ الْعَنِ التَّابِعَ وَالْمَتْبُوعَ، أَللّٰهُمَّ عَلَيْكَ بِالْأُقَيْعَسِ، قَالَ إِبْنُ الْبَرَاءِ لِأَبِيهِ: مَنِ الْأُقَيْعَسُ؟ قَالَ: مُعَاوِيَةُ.

and the way in which Muḥammad ibn Abī Bakr addressed him was as follows: "You are the imprecated and the son of the imprecated – both you and your father rose up in rebellion and insurrection against the Messenger of Allah ﷺ and both of you sought to extinguish the light of Allah."[39]

Regarding an individual named Naʿimān or Nuʿmān, it has been mentioned that he was one who imbibed alcohol and was even given the legal punishment in Islam [for drinking alcohol] many times while the Messenger of Allah ﷺ was present. It has been noted in the historical texts that: "Some of the companions said: 'May the malediction of Allah be upon him due to these excesses seen from him...'"[40]

After a certain event which took place, Abū Mūsā al-Ashʿarī said to ʿUmrū ʿĀṣ: "'May the imprecation of Allah be upon you as your similitude is that of a dog; if you go towards him, he sticks out his tongue; and if you leave him alone, he still sticks out his tongue. ʿUmrū ʿĀṣ replied to him: 'May the imprecation of Allah be upon you and indeed your similitude is like the example of a donkey carrying a heavy weight upon itself!'"[41]

---

[39] *Murūj al-Dhahab*, Vol. 1, Pg. 352; *Ansāb al-Ashrāf*, Vol. 1, Pg. 351; *Waqaʿat al-Ṣiffīn*, Vol. 1, Pg. 119; *Sharh Nahj al-Balāghah*, Vol. 3, Pg. 189:

أَنْتَ اللَّعِينُ بْنُ اللَّعِينِ، لَمْ تَزَلْ أَنْتَ وَأَبُوكَ تَبْغِيَانِ لِرَسُولِ اللهِ (صَلَّى اللهُ عَلَيْهِ وَآلِهِ) الْغَوَائِلِ، وَتَجْهُدَانِ فِي أَطْفَاءَ نُورُ اللهِ.

[40] *Iḥyā al-ʿUlūm al-Dīn*, Vol. 3, Pg. 162. This *ḥadīth* has also been mentioned in *Ṣaḥīḥ al-Bukhārī* and *al-Istīʿāb*:

قَالَ بَعْضُ الصَّحَابِهِ: لَعَنَهُ اللهُ مَا أَكْثَرَ مَا يُؤْتِي بِهِ.

[41] *ʿUqd al-Farīd*, Vol. 4, Pg. 146; *History of Ṭabarī*, Vol. 3, Pg. 313; *Al-Kāmil fīl Tārīkh*, Vol. 3, Pg. 158; *Bidāyah wa Nihāyah*, Vol. 7, Pg. 248:

لَعَنَكَ اللهُ فَإِنَّ مَثَلَكَ كَمَثَلِ الْكَلْبِ. إِنْ تَحْمِلْ عَلَيْهِ يَلْهَثْ أَوْ تَتْرُكْهُ يَلْهَثْ. قَالَ عُمْرُو: لَعَنَكَ اللهُ فَإِنَّ مَثَلَكَ كَمَثَلِ الْحِمَارِ يَحْمِلُ أَسْفَارًا.

In addition, even ʿUmar ibn al-Khaṭṭāb imprecated against Khālid ibn Walīd when he killed Mālik ibn Nuwayrah.[42]

Finally, we see that ʿAbdullāh ibn ʿUmar imprecated three times against his own son.[43]

The Ahl as-Sunnah and Malediction

One of the most significant proofs from some of the Ahl as-Sunnah in their rejection of malediction is their belief in defending the honour and integrity of all the companions since they consider the companions as being the prime sources of Islamic religious legislation alongside the *Quran*, *Sunnah*, *Ijmāʿ* (consensus) and *ʿaql* (intellect), and the other sources.

Sometimes, it is even seen that the ways and customs *(madhab)* of the companions is referred to as the *sunnah* of the companions and this clearly shows that the *sunnah* of the companions as well, is on the same horizontal plane as the *sunnah* of Prophet Muḥammad ﷺ for the Ahl as-Sunnah and that they too have a *sunnah* [just as it is an obligation to follow the *sunnah* of Prophet Muḥammad ﷺ so too for some people, it is an obligation to follow the *sunnah* of the companions].

They truly believe that if the companions are open to examination and analysis or are maledicted against, then this may lead to the instability of Islam, whereas a faith whose fundamentals has been laid down by Allah, the Highest, and the Noble Prophet Muḥammad ﷺ, and as has been promised by Allah ﷻ, will remain until the Day of Judgement, can never be made instable by the analysis and criticism of a few individuals!

---

[42] *History of Ṭabarī*, Vol. 2, Pg. 241 as narrated in the book, *Shīʿā Shināsī wa Pāsukh bi Shubuhāt*, Pg. 594

[43] *Jāmiʿ al-Bayān al-ʿIlm wa Fadhluhu*, Vol. 16, Pg. 414, Tradition 45174 as narrated in the book, *Shīʿā Shināsī wa Pāsukh bi Shubuhāt*, Pg. 594.

Thus, this belief that the *madhab* of the companions is one of the fundamental sources of Islamic legislation must also be rejected!

In this regard, Imam al-Ghazālī said: "The person, in whom there is a possibility of error and mistakes and whose infallibility from sins and faults is not proven, his statements are not a testimony or proof over us, therefore how can anyone ever rely on his testimony if he is prone to error!? In addition, how is it possible that without any successive proofs, one can claim infallibility of such individuals? In addition, how is it possible to imagine that a community of individuals would never have any differences of opinion amongst themselves, and even more, how is it possible that two infallible people would ever differ amongst themselves - whereas we see that there is a consensus amongst all the companions that one is permitted to go against the opinions of the other companions. Why is it that Abū Bakr and ʿUmar never allowed anyone, by way of their own independent assessment *(ijtihād)*, to differ with them; rather, in issues which call for *ijtihād*, it is an obligation upon every individual who has reached the level of being able to conduct independent research and analysis *(mujtahid)* to follow his own *ijtihad!*"[44]

Al-Shokānī, apparently in discussing the sources of Islamic legislation, has raised an objection, and has said that the opinions of the companions are not a proof [for us] as Allah only appointed Prophet Muḥammad ﷺ for this nation and other than one Prophet and one Divinely sent book, we have nothing else [to take as a proof of the religion].

Thus, he contends that the entire Muslim nation is obligated to follow and obey the Book of Allah (Quran) and the *sunnah* of Prophet Muḥammad ﷺ and there is no differentiation between

[44] *Al-Muṣṭafā*, Vol. 1, Pg. 135.

the companions or others as everyone is mandated to take their religious responsibilities from the Book and the *sunnah*.

Therefore, whoever says that after the Quran and the *sunnah* of the Prophet ﷺ and whatever reaches back to these two sources as a proof [of the religion] for us in the religion of Allah ﷻ, that there are other proofs [of legislation] has said something about the religion of Allah ﷻ which is incorrect.[45]

Therefore, the only things which are a proof over us [in terms of religious mandate] are the Quran, *sunnah* of the Prophet ﷺ, the unanimous consensus of the Muslim scholars, and the unambiguous intellect and the opinions of the companions – as long as their opinions **do not** go against the statements of the Prophet ﷺ - for if it goes against the Quran and *sunnah* then it is definitely not a proof of the religion for us; however, if their opinions are extracted and deduced from the Islamic religious sources, then for them and for those who follow them, they are a proof – and they are not binding on other people – on the *mujtahidīn* and the *muqallidīn*.

The companions of Prophet Muḥammad ﷺ and the first generation after the companions, are divided into two groups: righteous and iniquitous; and accepted and rejected; and when we do not accept the traditions which they claim to have heard Prophet Muḥammad ﷺ say, then we must clarify the point that this is not a condemnation that we reject all the traditions which the companions of the Prophet ﷺ related.

More than this, the traditions of the Prophet ﷺ which have been narrated by the infallible successors of the Prophet ﷺ - meaning ʿAlī ibn Abī Ṭālib ؑ and his family and noble line of successors who were indeed the best of companions of the Prophet ﷺ are at our disposal and we accept them. But we do not accept just any tradition narrated by individuals who are

[45] *Irshād al-Fuḥūl*, Pg. 214.

unconvincing or completely unknown. This is evidence that we do not reject all statements, nor does this bring any uncertainty to the faith as the Noble Prophet ﷺ left behind two valuable and solid arguments for the Muslim nation and by holding firmly onto both, we will be free from need of everything else.

The Wisdom Behind Malediction

Just as was previously explained, Islam has placed immense importance on love and hate to such an extent that in the traditions it has been mentioned that: "Is true faith anything other than love and hate!?"[46]

This love and hate have also been clearly manifested within Islamic history regarding specific individuals [and is not just a theory]. For example, Prophet Muḥammad ﷺ addressed the Commander of the Faithful ʿAlī (ع) and said: "O ʿAlī! Love for you is [a sign of] true faith and enmity of you is [a sign of] hypocrisy and disbelief."[47]

Regarding the wisdom and proofs on the emphasis and importance in Islam on the traits of love and hate – whether this be of a general nature or in relation to specific individuals, we will suffice with mentioning the following brief points:

1. We should keep in mind that love and hate are two extremely powerful forces within a person and that if they are allowed to fully surround a person's presence, then they will prove to reward a person with great benefits. For example, having love for a person since they have all the traits of goodness within

---

[46] *Biḥār al-Anwār*, Vol. 66, Pg. 241:

هَلِ الإِيـمَانُ إلاَّ الْحُبُّ وَ الْبُغْضُ.

[47] *Maʿānī al-Akhbār*, Pg. 206:

يَا عَلِيُّ، حُبُّكَ إِيـمَانٌ وَبُغْضُكَ نِفَاقٌ وَكُفْرٌ.

them is a show of the person's overwhelming possession of love and affinity to the totality of goodness, and this affection and passion which one has can prove to be an extremely powerful force which can take over one's entire essence and guide an individual towards the True Love – meaning Allah ﷻ. This is the meaning of the seeking of perfection and felicity for a human being. In addition, if a person shows enmity for an individual due to that person being wicked and evil, then this should lead to the person having one's entire presence covered with the detestation of all evil and bad which is possible, and this is the actual meaning of the distancing from corruption on a whole.

2. Contrary to some of the other global religions, Islam looks at the world as a two-sided coin - such that due to the societal requirements, the believers have been enjoined to keep in mind the two important beliefs of love and hate. A person is not able to have an affinity for both good and bad, or the manifestations of both good and bad within himself, as these two traits are opposite of one another and cannot be twinned and if they are seen in a person, then this is a sign of hypocrisy.
3. From the psychological aspect, it has also been proven that the best way (generally and specifically speaking) to encourage people towards following the truth and keeping away from corruption and bad deeds is to present them with the best and most perfect examples of both sides of the spectrum as this will have the desired outcome intended for a society.
4. It must be noted that love and hate cannot simply remain "in the heart." Rather, they must become manifest, and if their manifestation has no problems from being conducted – both from the point of view of the religious legal limits and from the rational aspect, then not only is it not a problem to

manifest these two states, rather, it becomes something extremely beneficial. This too can be proven from a psychological point of view as the display of a phenomenon leads to that thing being suggested and implanted into the spiritual heart and soul of a person – leading to an eventual state in which that thing becomes second-nature for an individual. It is for this reason that the application of love and hate, in the formation of the spiritual foundation of a person, plays a significant role.

5. Voicing our love and hate and showing malediction – which is one of the forms of voicing hatred – is the announcement of an impending hazard and the pronouncement of good news; the proclamation of hazard to the masses that they must be aware and on guard from the enemies of their religion – enemies who are constantly in wait, hoping to snatch a person's faith away and to misguide them from the straight path. Know that such people have been maledicted against and are not the kinds of people whom we should be following. Expressing our love is a form of announcement of good news to the people that they should know that we have perfect and flawless examples and if we follow them, then we will reach to the Truth and that we will eventually make it towards the Divine, and this is in reality, one of the manifestations of enjoining the good and forbidding the evil *(al-amr bil maʿrūf wa nahī ʿanil munkar)* on a societal level.
6. Due to certain reasons, the companions of Prophet Muḥammad ﷺ hold a special status because they are people who had seen the Prophet ﷺ; they heard him speak and they listened to the statements which he made, and they saw firsthand the way that he led his life. From another point of view, due to the self-sacrifice which some of them offered in the protection and spreading of the religion of Islam, they are worthy of having our respect, and it is for this reason that the

Muslims pay special attention to them. From a unique perspective, those people who truly tried to prevent the advancement and were the reason for misguidedness within the Islamic society enacted the greatest damage to Islam and the Muslims. It is for this reason that we must differentiate between the good and bad role models which exist amongst the midst of the companions of Prophet Muḥammad ﷺ - and the measuring stick for judging them is the primary role model which we all have – the Messenger of Allah ﷺ - just as Allah ﷻ says in the Qur'ān:

﴿لَقَدْ كَانَ لَكُمْ فِي رَسُولِ اللَّهِ أُسْوَةٌ حَسَنَةٌ...﴾

Indeed, in the Messenger of Allah [Muḥammad] is the best role model for you...[48]

Malediction and Muslim Unity

Just as was previously shown, the historical reports demonstrate to us that some major individuals around the Messenger of Allah ﷺ - people such as Muʿāwiyah, ʿUmrū ibn ʿĀṣ, Khālid ibn Walīd, Ziyād and Ḥajjāj ibn Yūsuf had all evoked malediction (upon others). In addition, the day that ʿUthmān was killed, Imam ʿAlī عليه السلام also imprecated against and evoked malediction against ʿAbdullāh ibn Zubayr as he did not stand up to defend ʿUthmān.[49]

It is not possible for today's generation of Muslims, those who want to traverse the path of goodness, dignity, and moral refinement, to shut their eyes to the historical legacy which they have inherited, and only partially study the situation of the earlier groups of Muslims. If history is supposed to be the mirror for learning lessons and gaining experiences (from what has

[48] Quran, Sūrah al-Aḥzāb (33), Verse 21.
[49] *Murūj al-Dhahab*, Vol. 2, Pg. 54.

transpired), then one who wants to take a lesson from the past cannot help but reflect on what has gone by.

Thus, the art of evoking malediction and imprecation as a mechanism for expressing one's revulsion and aversion towards the epitome of foulness, plays a great role in the strengthening of a believer's inner beliefs and spiritual soul; and by not giving this importance and taking the issue lightly by being indifferent to the matter will result in a person being easily able to trespass beyond the borders of the religious and ethical aura.

Of course, naturally when a believer studies the unadulterated pages of history, one will see the manifestations of hypocrisy, oppression, and misguidedness and this should fill one with detest towards those historical criminals.

Certainly, we must keep the following point in mind that when it comes to specific individuals, one must be careful that one only evokes malediction upon those for whom there are solid arguments that clearly indicate that within those individuals existed the traits which would validate the evoking of malediction upon them. In instances of questionable ethical traits [which they may or may not have displayed] one must be sure to evoke malediction upon such people only after proof has been established, as it is not permissible that one conducts this action except with solid proofs. Therefore, evoking malediction upon the companions of the Prophet ﷺ who have not shown any proofs for them to be imprecated against will bring about damage to the unity of the Muslims.

In addition, it must also be noted that rather than resorting to exaggeration when it comes to evoking malediction in the religious gatherings and in the various forms of mass media, one should instead make use of rational arguments which are impartial and balanced and are backed up with proofs (from the Islamic texts), and that this should be the sort of culture which is spread throughout the masses [meaning using logical discussions and debates rather than just the act of mere malediction].

There is no greater interest over the convergence and unity of the Muslims with one another which can be imaged which would necessitate that the usage of any coarse and abrasive words of disparagement against the revered personalities of most of the Muslims. Therefore, everyone must think in this same way and keep away from any sort of discussions on the sidelines [which would bring about ill feelings amongst the Muslims]. Through practical steps, we should lay down a course for the advancement of the principal goals of Islam and the Muslims and indeed the best and most practical example which we have is embodied in the life history of the Infallibles ﷺ as they show us the best examples that we need for us to traverse this path. In addition, by reviewing the ways of the Commander of the Faithful ʿAlī ibn Abī Ṭālib ﷺ, we see points of guidance which he was able to convey to the second caliph, ʿUmar – all of which were done simply to protect and strengthen Islam and the Muslims.

In the book, *Mustadrak ʿalā al-Ṣaḥīḥḥayn*, as narrated by Saʿīd ibn Musayyab it has been mentioned that: "ʿUmar gathered the people together and asked them: 'From what day should we start the calendar [of the Muslims]?' Each of the people present gave their own opinions however ʿUmar was not satisfied with what he heard. At that time, ʿAlī ibn Abī Ṭālib ﷺ said: 'Start the Muslim calendar from the day that the Messenger of Allah migrated and left the land of polytheism [Mecca].'" ʿUmar accepted his suggestion and thus the Islamic calendar began with the *hijrah* – the migration to Medina."[50]

[50] *Mustadrak ʿalā al-Ṣaḥīḥḥayn*, Vol. 3, Pg. 3,287; *Al-Tārikh al-Kabīr*, Vol. 1, Pg. 9; *Tārikh* of al-Ṭabarī, Vol. 4, Pg. 39; *Tārikh al-Madīnah*, Vol. 2, Pg. 758; *al-Iqbāl*, Vol. 3, Pg. 22; *al-Manāqib*, Vol. 2, Pg. 144 – all of these have been referenced from the book *al-Tanbīat al-Ashrāf*, Pg. 252.

In the book, *al-Bidāyah wa al-Nihāyah*, it has been cited that when ʿUmar wanted to date writings which had been done up until that point, he wished to start [Islamic] history from the date of the birth of the Prophet of Allah ﷺ. Later, he changed his mind and said that he would start it from the *biʿthah* (the official appointment of Prophet Muḥammad ﷺ to prophethood). At this point in time, ʿAlī ibn Abī Ṭālib ؑ gave his opinion that they should take the *Hijrah* or migration from Mecca to Medina as the starting point to which ʿUmar agreed and began to use this date in his writings.[51]

In the book, *The History of Ṭabarī,* as narrated by Ibn ʿUmar, it has been mentioned that after the conquest of Qādisiyyah and Damishq (The Levant), ʿUmar (b. Al-Khaṭṭāb) gathered the people in Medina together and said to them: "In your opinion, how much wealth from the public treasury should I be allowed to use on my own personal self?' Those present each spoke out with an opinion, however ʿAlī ؑ remained silent. ʿUmar said: 'O ʿAlī! What do you think?' To this, ʿAlī ؑ replied: 'Only that amount which brings about ease for you and your family and other than this, there is no more wealth from the public treasury which is permissible for you.' Everyone present replied: 'The [correct] opinion is that of ʿAlī ibn Abī Ṭālib.'"[52]

In addition, in the book *Rabīʿ al-Abrār* it has been mentioned that: "During the era of the reign of ʿUmar ibn al-Khaṭṭāb, a discussion once ensued in his presence regarding the numerous precious, expensive chains which were upon the *Kaʿbah*, used as decorations. A group of people said to him: 'If we were to sell them and use that money to mobilize and equip the Muslim army,

---

[51] *Tārikh al-Yaʿqūbī*, Vol. 2, Pg. 145; *Al-Bidāyah wal Nihāyah*, Vol. 7, Pg. 74.

[52] *Tārikh Ṭabarī*, Vol. 3, Pg. 616; *Al-Kāmil fīl Tārikh*, Vol. 2, Pg. 135; *Commentary of Nahj al-Balāghah*, Vol. 12, Pg. 220.

the reward would be much greater [than just having them hang on the Ka'bah]. What need does the Ka'bah have for these chains!?' 'Umar took the decision to do as others suggested and to take the chains on the Ka'bah and sell them, however 'Alī ؏ said to him: 'This Quran was revealed to the Prophet ﷺ and at that time, there were four forms of income which were expressly spoken about: the first is the inheritance of the Muslims (and amongst the inheritors who are entitled to a portion, one is Allah); the second is the *khums* (which Allah has mentioned in the Quran); the third is the *zakāt* (which Allah has also specifically spoken about and has also mentioned how this wealth should be used); the fourth are the chains of the Ka'bah which were present even in that day [during the era of the Prophet ﷺ] – however Allah left them as they were and did not speak about them – not because He forgot to mention them and not because these were hidden from the sight and knowledge of Allah. Thus, you need not think about those chains - just leave them where they are – just as Allah and His Prophet did.' 'Umar replied and said: 'If you were not here, we would have been disgraced.' Following this, he ['Umar] left the chains as they were.'"[53]

Of course it must be noted that the Commander of the Faithful 'Alī ؏ working with 'Umar and giving him advise was not a sign of Imam 'Alī ؏ accepting 'Umar's caliphate – rather, it was only done to save the faith of Islam and the Muslims, as it can be seen that during the periods of the caliphate of Abū Bakr, 'Umar and 'Uthmān, he continued to emphasize on his own truthfulness to the seat of caliphate and him being the rightful successor of the Messenger of Allah ﷺ.

As an example, during the event of the 'consultative assembly' that 'Umar devised to choose his own successor, in one of Imam

---

[53] *Nahj al-Balāghah*, wise saying 270; *Al-Manāqib*, Vol. 2, Pg. 368; *Rabī al-Abrār*, Vol. 4, Pg. 26.

ʿAlī's sermons in regards to the outcome of this assembly he stated: "Nevertheless, I remained patient despite length of period and stiffness of trial, until when he went his way (of death) he put the matter (of caliphate) in a group and regarded me to be one of them. But good heavens! What had I to do with this "consultation"? Where was any doubt about me about the first of them that I was now considered akin to these ones? But I remained low when they were low and flew high when they flew high. One of them turned against me because of his hatred and the other got inclined the other way due to his in-law relationship and this thing and that thing, until the third man of these people stood up with heaving breasts between his dung and fodder."[54]

In addition, it has been mentioned in the commentary of *Nahj al-Balāgha* that Imam ʿAlī said the following to Ibn ʿAbbās: 'It is for this reason that I entered that gathering of the 'consultative assembly' [to decide on the next caliph] as before this, 'Umar had said that he heard the Prophet of Allah say, '*Nubuwwah* and *Imāmah* will never be combined in one house.' I went into this consultative assembly just to show the people his contradictory

---

[54] *Nahj al-Balāghah*, Sermon 3; *Al-Irshād*, Vol. 1, Pg. 287; *Maʿānī al-Akhbār*, Pg. 361, Tradition 1; *'Ilal ash-Sharāʾiʿ*, Pg. 150, Tradition 12; *Al-Amālī* of Shaykh al-Ṭūsī, Pg. 372; Al-Iḥtijāj, Vol. 1, Pg. 452, Tradition 105; *Al-Manāqib*, Vol. 2, Pg. 204; *Nadhr al-Durr*, Vol. 1, Pg. 274; *Tadhkirat al-Khawwāṣ*, Pg. 124:

فَصَبَرْتُ عَلَى طُولِ الْمُدَّةِ، وَشِدَّةِ الْمحْنَةِ، حَتَّى إِذا مَضَى لِسَبِيلِهِ جَعَلَهَا في جَمَاعَة زَعَمَ أَنِّي أَحَدُهُمْ .فَيَاللهِ وَلِلشُّورَى! مَتَى اعْتَرَضَ الرَّيْبُ فِيَّ مَعَ الأوَّلِ مِنْهُمْ، حَتَّى صِرْتُ أُقْرَنُ إِلَى هذِهِ النَّظَائِرِ! لكِنِّي أسففْتُ إِذْ أَسَفُّوا، وَطِرْتُ إِذْ طَارُوا، فَصَغَا رَجُلُ مِنْهُمْ لِضِغْنِه، وَمَالَ الأخَرُ لِصِهْرِهِ، مَعَ هَن وَهَن. إِلَى أَنْ قَامَ ثَالِثُ القَوْمِ، نَافِجاً حِضْنَيْهِ بَيْنَ نَثِيلهِ وَمُعْتَلَفِهِ،

actions with the (supposed) statement [from the Noble Prophet] which he was claiming.'"⁵⁵

In addition, it has also been mentioned in *Nahj al-Balāgha* that ʿAlī ؏ said the following to ʿAbd al-Raḥmān ibn ʿAwf: "You have certainly known that I am the most rightful of all others for the Caliphate. By Allah, so long as the affairs of Muslims remain intact and there is no oppression in it save on myself, I shall keep quiet seeking reward for it (from Allah) and keeping aloof from its attractions and allurements for which you aspire."⁵⁶

It has been mentioned in the book, *Al-Irshād*, as narrated by Jundab ibn ʿAbdullāh that the latter said: I visited ʿAlī ibn Abī Ṭālib ؏ in Medina after the people had given the pledge of allegiance to ʿUthmān. I found him with head lowered and sorrowful. I asked him: "What has come upon your people?"

"Beautiful endurance," he answered.

"Praise be to Allah!" I said. "By Allah, you are indeed enduring. Do what you said you would do among the people. Summon them to yourself and inform them that you are the closest and most appropriate of the people by virtue (of your relationship) with the Prophet ﷺ by virtue of your outstanding merit *(faḍl)* and your priority (in Islam). Ask them to help you against these men who have conspired against you. If ten out of a hundred answer you, you would be a powerful influence with the ten over the hundred. If they approached you, that would be as you would want. If they refused, you could fight them. If you are victorious, then the authority is Allah's, Who gave it to his

---

⁵⁵ *Commentary on Nahj al-Balāghah*, Vol. 1, Pg. 189.
⁵⁶ *Nahj al-Balāghah*, Sermon 74:

لَقَدْ عَلِمْتُمْ أَنِّي أَحَقُّ بِهَا مِنْ غَيْرِي، وَوَاللهِ لَأَسْلِمَنَّ مَاسَلِمَتْ أُمُورُ الْمُسْلِمِينَ، وَلَمْ يَكُنْ فِيهَا جَوْرٌ إِلاَّ عَلَيَّ خَاصَّةً، الْتِمَاساً لِاجْرِ ذلِكَ وَفَضْلِهِ، وَزُهْداً فِيَما تَنَافَسْتُمُوهُ مِنْ زُخْرُفِهِ وَزِبْرِجِهِ

Prophet ﷺ and you are more appropriate for it than them. If you are killed in seeking it, then you would be killed as a martyr and you would be more deserving of Allah's forgiveness and have more right to the inheritance of the Apostle of Allah ﷺ."

"Jundub," he said, "do you think that ten out of a hundred would pledge allegiance to me?"

"I would hope so," I replied.

"However," he retorted, "I do not expect two men from every hundred. I will tell you why. The people look to Quraysh. Quraysh says that the family of Muḥammad think that they have merit over the rest of the people and that they are the masters *(awliyāʾ)* of the affair apart from (the rest of) Quraysh. (They say that) if they took charge of it, this authority would never leave them to go to anyone else. Since it is already with others, you should circulate it among yourselves. No, by Allah, Quraysh will never give this authority to us voluntarily."

"Won't you go back and tell the people what you have just said?" I asked him. "Then summon them to yourself."

"Jundub," he said, "this is not the time for that."

After that, I returned to Iraq. Whenever I used to mention any of his virtues, accomplishments, and rights to the people, they would treat me roughly and drive me away until the matter of my words was brought before al-Walīd b. ʿUqbā who was our governor at that time. He sent for me and imprisoned me until someone spoke to him about me and then he freed me."[57]

---

57 *Al-Irshād*, Vol. 1, Pg. 241:

دَخَلْتُ عَلَى عَلِيِّ بْنِ أَبِي طَالِبٍ بِالْمَدِينَةِ بَعْدَ بَيْعَةِ النَّاسِ لِعُثْمَانَ فَوَجَدْتُهُ مُطْرِقًا كَئِيبًا فَقُلْتُ لَهُ: مَا أَصَابَ قَوْمَكَ؟

قَالَ صَبْرٌ جَمِيلٌ.

فَقُلْتُ لَهُ: سُبْحَانَ اللهِ وَاللهِ إِنَّكَ لَصَبُورٌ.

Conclusion

From all of that which has been mentioned, we reach to this conclusion that the issue of love and hate and specifically the act of malediction is not only something which is allowed in Islam, rather, it is one of the societal requirements and is one of the ways to encourage people towards the truth and realities of Islam, and it is a mechanism by way the masses are kept away from corruption and destruction. How is it possible that a person refrains from renouncing those who are worthy of being repudiated whereas Allah, the Highest, says in the Quran:

قَالَ: فَأَصْنَعُ مَا ذَا فَقُلْتُ تَقُومُ فِي النَّاسِ وَتَدْعُوهُمْ إِلَى نَفْسِكَ وَتُخْبِرُهُمْ أَنَّكَ أَوْلَى بِالنَّبِيِّ ﷺ بِالْفَضْلِ وَالسَّابِقَةِ وَتَسْأَلُهُمُ النَّصْرَ عَلَى هَؤُلَاءِ الْمُتَمَالِئِينَ عَلَيْكَ فَإِنْ أَجَابَكَ عَشَرَةٌ مِنْ مِائَةٍ شَدَّدْتَ بِالْعَشَرَةِ عَلَى الْمِائَةِ وَإِنْ دَانُوا لَكَ كَانَ ذٰلِكَ عَلَى مَا أَحْبَبْتَ وَإِنْ أَبَوْا قَاتَلْتَهُمْ فَإِنْ ظَهَرْتَ عَلَيْهِمْ فَهُوَ سُلْطَانُ اللهِ الَّذِي آتَاهُ نَبِيَّهُ ﷺ وَكُنْتَ أَوْلَى بِهِ مِنْهُمْ وَإِنْ قُتِلْتَ فِي طَلَبِهِ قُتِلْتَ شَهِيدًا وَكُنْتَ أَوْلَى بِالْعُذْرِ عِنْدَ اللهِ وَأَحَقَّ بِمِيرَاثِ رَسُولِ اللَّهِ ﷺ.

فَقَالَ: أَ تَرَاهُ يَا جُنْدَبُ يُبَايِعُنِي عَشَرَةٌ مِنْ مِائَةٍ قُلْتُ أَرْجُو ذٰلِكَ.

قَالَ: لَكِنَّنِي لَا أَرْجُو وَلَا مِنْ كُلِّ مِائَةٍ اثْنَيْنِ وَسَأُخْبِرُكَ مِنْ أَيْنَ ذٰلِكَ إِنَّمَا يَنْظُرُ النَّاسُ إِلَى قُرَيْشٍ وَإِنَّ قُرَيْشًا تَقُولُ إِنَّ آلَ مُحَمَّدٍ يَرَوْنَ أَنَّ لَهُمْ فَضْلًا عَلَى سَائِرِ النَّاسِ وَأَنَّهُمْ أَوْلِيَاءُ الْأَمْرِ دُونَ قُرَيْشٍ وَإِنَّهُمْ إِنْ وُلُّوهُ لَمْ يَخْرُجْ مِنْهُمْ هٰذَا السُّلْطَانُ إِلَى أَحَدٍ أَبَدًا وَمَتَى كَانَ فِي غَيْرِهِمْ تَدَاوَلْتُمُوهُ بَيْنَكُمْ وَلَا وَاللهِ لَا تَدْفَعُ قُرَيْشٌ إِلَيْنَا هٰذَا السُّلْطَانَ طَائِعِينَ أَبَدًا.

قَالَ: فَقُلْتُ لَهُ: أَ فَلَا أَرْجِعُ فَأُخْبِرُ النَّاسَ بِمَقَالَتِكَ هٰذِهِ وَأَدْعُوهُمْ إِلَيْكَ.

فَقَالَ لِي: يَا جُنْدَبُ لَيْسَ هٰذَا زَمَانَ ذٰلِكَ.

قَالَ: فَرَجَعْتُ بَعْدَ ذٰلِكَ إِلَى الْعِرَاقِ فَكُنْتُ كُلَّمَا ذَكَرْتُ لِلنَّاسِ شَيْئًا مِنْ فَضَائِلِ عَلِيِّ بْنِ أَبِي طَالِبٍ عليه السلام وَمَنَاقِبِهِ وَحُقُوقِهِ زَبَرُونِي وَنَهَرُونِي حَتَّى رُفِعَ ذٰلِكَ مِنْ قَوْلِي إِلَى الْوَلِيدِ بْنِ عُقْبَةَ لَيَالِيَ وَلِيَنَا فَبَعَثَ إِلَيَّ فَحَبَسَنِي حَتَّى كُلِّمَ فِيَّ فَخَلَّى سَبِيلِي.

﴿قَدْ كَانَتْ لَكُمْ أُسْوَةٌ حَسَنَةٌ فِي إِبْرَاهِيمَ وَالَّذِينَ مَعَهُ إِذْ قَالُوا لِقَوْمِهِمْ إِنَّا بُرَآءُ مِنْكُمْ وَمِمَّا تَعْبُدُونَ مِنْ دُونِ اللهِ كَفَرْنَا بِكُمْ وَبَدَا بَيْنَنَا وَبَيْنَكُمُ الْعَدَاوَةُ وَالْبَغْضَآءُ أَبَداً﴾

> There is certainly a good exemplar for you in Abraham and those who were with him, when they said to their own people, 'Indeed we repudiate you and whatever you worship besides Allah. We disavow you, and between you and us there has appeared enmity and hate forever....[58]

However it must be noted that some companions of the Messenger of Allah ﷺ - meaning those who accepted the call to Islam and went through extreme pressures while in Mecca and resorted to various means in order to safeguard their religion, and even the Muslims who after the migration to Medina shed their blood to water this new-sapling called Islam in the initial wars, as well as the individuals who after the death of the Messenger of Allah ﷺ said farewell to their homes and possessions and went forth in the sacred struggle – all of these groups of individuals are to be congratulated, honoured and respected. Like a candle, they "burnt" while trying to give light to their surroundings – and no Muslims have a difference of opinion regarding these self-sacrificing individuals, who were true and noble companions.

Rather, the debate and examination are regarding the other companions of the Prophet ﷺ - because they were not flawless. When they intentionally performed a sin and fit into the criteria for one who is worthy of having malediction evoked upon them – then what is the religious ruling on passing judgement over such individuals?

Naturally, the ruling of such people, as it would be for anyone other than them who are in the same position of committing such

---

[58] Quran, Sūrah al-Mumtaḥana (60), Verse 4.

an act is the same [and thus they should and must be open to critique and criticism when they are openly and intentionally violet the Islamic laws].

Therefore, if the Shīʿa seek to distance themselves from an identifiable group of "companions" of the Noble Prophet ﷺ then it is not because they are considered as "companions"; rather, evoking the malediction of Allah ﷻ upon this limited group of individuals known as the "companions" is due to the fact that even though they saw the Prophet ﷺ, and were able to benefit from him and his magnanimous status, however they actively and consciously decided to stay in their state of spiritual negligence and to act against the orders and commandments of the Noble Prophet ﷺ such that they deserve that the Muslims distance themselves from them – as the Noble Quran has stated:

﴿إِنَّ ٱلَّذِينَ يُؤۡذُونَ ٱللَّهَ وَرَسُولَهُۥ لَعَنَهُمُ ٱللَّهُ فِي ٱلدُّنۡيَا وَٱلۡأٓخِرَةِ وَأَعَدَّ لَهُمۡ عَذَابٗا مُّهِينٗا ٥٧﴾

> Indeed, those who torment Allah, and His Apostle are cursed by Allah in this world and in the Hereafter, and He has prepared a humiliating punishment for them.[59]

Therefore, if one of the "companions" of Prophet Muḥammad ﷺ did something which led to the Prophet ﷺ being tormented, then that companion would be found guilty of the infraction mentioned in the verse quoted above, just like if anyone other than one of the companions was to possess any of the traits which would make him worthy of having the mercy of Allah ﷻ be removed from him. Further, he too would be worthy of having the malediction of Allah ﷻ inflicted upon him – and of course in Islam, there is no discrimination when it comes to such things – all are equal in front of the law.

---

[59] Quran, Sūrah al-Aḥzāb (33), Verse 57.

It is with this said that the Shīʿa employ the concept of evoking the malediction of Allah ﷻ upon certain "companions" who were sources of corruption in the Muslim society - not only during their own era, but even after they left this world and up until the Day of Judgement.

The Quran and Malediction

We can divide the verses of the Quran which speak about malediction, which come up around 44 times, into six main categories:

1. Malediction against Satan

﴿وَإِنَّ عَلَيْكَ ٱللَّعْنَةَ إِلَىٰ يَوْمِ ٱلدِّينِ ٣٥﴾

And indeed, the curse shall lie on you until the Day of Retribution.[60]

﴿وَإِنَّ عَلَيْكَ لَعْنَتِيٓ إِلَىٰ يَوْمِ ٱلدِّينِ ٧٨﴾

And indeed, My curse will be on you until the Day of Retribution.[61]

﴿لَّعَنَهُ ٱللَّهُ وَقَالَ لَأَتَّخِذَنَّ مِنْ عِبَادِكَ نَصِيبًا مَّفْرُوضًا ١١٨﴾

Whom Allah has cursed, and who said, 'I will surely take of Your servants a settled share...[62]

---

[60] Quran, Sūrah al-Ḥijr (15), Verse 35.
[61] Ibid., Sūrah al-Ṣaad (38), Verse 78.
[62] Ibid., Sūrah al-Nisā (4), Verse 118.

2. Malediction against the Disbelievers

2.1 General Verses

﴿إِنَّ ٱللَّهَ لَعَنَ ٱلۡكَٰفِرِينَ وَأَعَدَّ لَهُمۡ سَعِيرًا ٦٤﴾

Indeed, Allah has cursed the faithless and prepared for them a blaze.[63]

﴿إِنَّ ٱلَّذِينَ كَفَرُواْ وَمَاتُواْ وَهُمۡ كُفَّارٌ أُوْلَٰٓئِكَ عَلَيۡهِمۡ لَعۡنَةُ ٱللَّهِ
وَٱلۡمَلَٰٓئِكَةِ وَٱلنَّاسِ أَجۡمَعِينَ ١٦١﴾

Indeed, those who turn faithless and die while they are faithless, —it is they on whom shall be the curse of Allah, the angels and all of humankind.[64]

﴿وَعَدَ ٱللَّهُ ٱلۡمُنَٰفِقِينَ وَٱلۡمُنَٰفِقَٰتِ وَٱلۡكُفَّارَ نَارَ جَهَنَّمَ خَٰلِدِينَ فِيهَاۚ
هِيَ حَسۡبُهُمۡۚ وَلَعَنَهُمُ ٱللَّهُۖ وَلَهُمۡ عَذَابٞ مُّقِيمٞ ٦٨﴾

Allah has promised the hypocrites, men, and women, and the faithless, the Fire of hell, to remain in it [forever]. That suffices them. Allah has cursed them, and there is a lasting punishment for them.[65]

---

63 Quran, Sūrah al-Aḥzāb (33), Verse 64.
64 Ibid., Sūrah al-Baqarah (2), Verse 161.
65 Ibid., Sūrah al-Tawbah (9), Verse 68.

2.2 Specific Verses – Those who Left the Faith

﴿كَيْفَ يَهْدِي ٱللَّهُ قَوْمًا كَفَرُواْ بَعْدَ إِيمَٰنِهِمْ وَشَهِدُوٓاْ أَنَّ ٱلرَّسُولَ حَقٌّ وَجَآءَهُمُ ٱلْبَيِّنَٰتُ ۚ وَٱللَّهُ لَا يَهْدِي ٱلْقَوْمَ ٱلظَّٰلِمِينَ ﴿٨٦﴾ أُوْلَٰٓئِكَ جَزَآؤُهُمْ أَنَّ عَلَيْهِمْ لَعْنَةَ ٱللَّهِ وَٱلْمَلَٰٓئِكَةِ وَٱلنَّاسِ أَجْمَعِينَ ﴿٨٧﴾﴾

How shall Allah guide a people who have disbelieved after their faith and [after] bearing witness that the Apostle is true, and [after] manifest proofs have come to them? Allah does not guide the wrongdoing people. Their requital is that there shall be upon them the curse of Allah, the angels, and all of humankind.[66]

2.3 Disbelievers from Amongst the Tribe of Ād

﴿وَأُتْبِعُواْ فِي هَٰذِهِ ٱلدُّنْيَا لَعْنَةً وَيَوْمَ ٱلْقِيَٰمَةِ ۗ أَلَآ إِنَّ عَادًا كَفَرُواْ رَبَّهُمْ ۗ أَلَا بُعْدًا لِّعَادٍ قَوْمِ هُودٍ ﴿٦٠﴾﴾

So, they were pursued by a curse in this world and on the Day of Resurrection. Look! Indeed, Ad defied their Lord. Look! Away with Ad, the people of Hud![67]

2.4 Disbelievers from Amongst the People of the Pharaoh

﴿وَأُتْبِعُواْ فِي هَٰذِهِۦ لَعْنَةً وَيَوْمَ ٱلْقِيَٰمَةِ ۚ بِئْسَ ٱلرِّفْدُ ٱلْمَرْفُودُ ﴿٩٩﴾﴾

[66] Quran, Sūrah Āl ʿImrān (3), verses 86 & 87.
[67] Ibid., Sūrah Hūd (11), Verse 60.

They were pursued by a curse in this [world], as well as on the Day of Resurrection; evil is the award conferred [upon them]![68]

﴿وَأَتْبَعْنَٰهُمْ فِي هَٰذِهِ ٱلدُّنْيَا لَعْنَةً ۖ وَيَوْمَ ٱلْقِيَٰمَةِ هُم مِّنَ
ٱلْمَقْبُوحِينَ ﴿٤٢﴾﴾

We made a curse pursue them in this world, and on the Day of Resurrection they will be among the disfigured.[69]

2.5 Disbelievers from Amongst the Tribes of Israel

﴿وَقَالُوا۟ قُلُوبُنَا غُلْفٌۢ ۚ بَل لَّعَنَهُمُ ٱللَّهُ بِكُفْرِهِمْ فَقَلِيلًا مَّا
يُؤْمِنُونَ ﴿٨٨﴾ وَلَمَّا جَآءَهُمْ كِتَٰبٌ مِّنْ عِندِ ٱللَّهِ مُصَدِّقٌ لِّمَا مَعَهُمْ
وَكَانُوا۟ مِن قَبْلُ يَسْتَفْتِحُونَ عَلَى ٱلَّذِينَ كَفَرُوا۟ فَلَمَّا جَآءَهُم مَّا
عَرَفُوا۟ كَفَرُوا۟ بِهِۦ ۚ فَلَعْنَةُ ٱللَّهِ عَلَى ٱلْكَٰفِرِينَ ﴿٨٩﴾﴾

They say: 'Our hearts are wrapped up in covers.' Rather Allah has cursed them for their unfaith, so few of them have faith. And when there came to them a Book from Allah, confirming that which is with them —and earlier they would pray for victory over the pagans—so when there came to them what they recognized, they defied it. So may the curse of Allah be upon the faithless![70]

﴿فَبِمَا نَقْضِهِم مِّيثَٰقَهُمْ لَعَنَّٰهُمْ وَجَعَلْنَا قُلُوبَهُمْ قَٰسِيَةً ۖ يُحَرِّفُونَ
ٱلْكَلِمَ عَن مَّوَاضِعِهِۦ ۙ وَنَسُوا۟ حَظًّا مِّمَّا ذُكِّرُوا۟ بِهِۦ ۚ وَلَا تَزَالُ تَطَّلِعُ

[68] Quran, Sūrah Hūd (11), Verse 99.
[69] Ibid., Sūrah al-Qaṣaṣ (28), Verse 42.
[70] Ibid., Sūrah al-Baqarah (2), verses 88 & 89.

عَلَىٰ خَآئِنَةٖ مِّنۡهُمۡ إِلَّا قَلِيلٗا مِّنۡهُمۡۖ فَٱعۡفُ عَنۡهُمۡ وَٱصۡفَحۡۚ إِنَّ ٱللَّهَ يُحِبُّ ٱلۡمُحۡسِنِينَ ﴿١٣﴾

Then, because of their breaking their covenant We cursed them and made their hearts hard: they pervert words from their meanings and have forgotten a part of what they were reminded. You will not cease to learn about some of their treachery, excepting a few of them. Yet excuse them and forbear. Indeed, Allah loves the virtuous.[71]

﴿قُلۡ هَلۡ أُنَبِّئُكُم بِشَرّٖ مِّن ذَٰلِكَ مَثُوبَةً عِندَ ٱللَّهِۚ مَن لَّعَنَهُ ٱللَّهُ وَغَضِبَ عَلَيۡهِ وَجَعَلَ مِنۡهُمُ ٱلۡقِرَدَةَ وَٱلۡخَنَازِيرَ وَعَبَدَ ٱلطَّٰغُوتَۚ أُوْلَٰٓئِكَ شَرّٞ مَّكَانٗا وَأَضَلُّ عَن سَوَآءِ ٱلسَّبِيلِ ﴿٦٠﴾

Say, 'Shall I inform you concerning something worse than that as a requital from Allah? Those whom Allah has cursed and with whom He is wrathful, and turned some of whom into apes and swine, and worshippers of the Rebel! Such are in a worse situation, and more astray from the right way.'[72]

﴿لُعِنَ ٱلَّذِينَ كَفَرُواْ مِنۢ بَنِيٓ إِسۡرَٰٓءِيلَ عَلَىٰ لِسَانِ دَاوُۥدَ وَعِيسَى ٱبۡنِ مَرۡيَمَۚ ذَٰلِكَ بِمَا عَصَواْ وَّكَانُواْ يَعۡتَدُونَ ﴿٧٨﴾

The faithless among the Children of Israel were cursed on the tongue of David and Jesus' son of Mary. That, because they would disobey and used to commit transgression.[73]

71 Quran, Sūrah al-Mā'idah (5), Verse 49.
72 Ibid., Sūrah al-Mā'idah (5), Verse 60.
73 Ibid, Verse 78.

﴿وَأُتۡبِعُواْ فِي هَٰذِهِۦ لَعۡنَةٗ وَيَوۡمَ ٱلۡقِيَٰمَةِۚ بِئۡسَ ٱلرِّفۡدُ ٱلۡمَرۡفُودُ ٩٩﴾

They were pursued by a curse in this [world], as well as on the Day of Resurrection; evil is the reward conferred [upon them]![74]

﴿وَأَتۡبَعۡنَٰهُمۡ فِي هَٰذِهِ ٱلدُّنۡيَا لَعۡنَةٗۖ وَيَوۡمَ ٱلۡقِيَٰمَةِ هُم مِّنَ
ٱلۡمَقۡبُوحِينَ ٤٢﴾

We made a curse pursue them in this world, and on the Day of Resurrection they will be among the disfigured.[75]

2.6 Disbelievers from Amongst the People of the Book

﴿وَلَمَّا جَآءَهُمۡ كِتَٰبٞ مِّنۡ عِندِ ٱللَّهِ مُصَدِّقٞ لِّمَا مَعَهُمۡ وَكَانُواْ مِن
قَبۡلُ يَسۡتَفۡتِحُونَ عَلَى ٱلَّذِينَ كَفَرُواْ فَلَمَّا جَآءَهُم مَّا عَرَفُواْ
كَفَرُواْ بِهِۦۚ فَلَعۡنَةُ ٱللَّهِ عَلَى ٱلۡكَٰفِرِينَ ٨٩﴾

And when there came to them a Book from Allah, confirming that which is with them—and earlier they would pray for victory over the pagans—so when there came to them what they recognized, they defied it. So may the curse of Allah be upon the faithless![76]

﴿مِّنَ ٱلَّذِينَ هَادُواْ يُحَرِّفُونَ ٱلۡكَلِمَ عَن مَّوَاضِعِهِۦ وَيَقُولُونَ سَمِعۡنَا
وَعَصَيۡنَا وَٱسۡمَعۡ غَيۡرَ مُسۡمَعٖ وَرَٰعِنَا لَيَّۢا بِأَلۡسِنَتِهِمۡ وَطَعۡنٗا فِي ٱلدِّينِۚ

---

[74] Quran, Sūrah Hūd (11), Verse 99.
[75] Ibid., Sūrah al-Qaṣaṣ (28), Verse 42.
[76] Ibid., Sūrah al-Baqarah (2), Verse 89.

وَلَوْ أَنَّهُمْ قَالُوا۟ سَمِعْنَا وَأَطَعْنَا وَٱسْمَعْ وَٱنظُرْنَا لَكَانَ خَيْرًا لَّهُمْ وَأَقْوَمَ
وَلَٰكِن لَّعَنَهُمُ ٱللَّهُ بِكُفْرِهِمْ فَلَا يُؤْمِنُونَ إِلَّا قَلِيلًا ﴿٤٦﴾

Among the Jews are those who pervert words from their meanings and say, 'We hear and disobey' and 'Hear without listening!' and 'Raʿinā,' twisting their tongues and reviling the faith. But had they said, 'We hear and obey' and 'Listen' and 'Unẓurnā,' it would have been better for them, and more upright. But Allah has cursed them for their lack of faith, so they will not believe except a few. O you who were given the Book! Believe in what We have sent down confirming what is with you, before We blot out the faces and turn them backwards or curse them as We cursed the People of the Sabbath, and Allah's command is bound to be fulfilled.[77]

﴿وَقَالَتِ ٱلْيَهُودُ يَدُ ٱللَّهِ مَغْلُولَةٌ ۚ غُلَّتْ أَيْدِيهِمْ وَلُعِنُوا۟ بِمَا قَالُوا۟ ۘ بَلْ
يَدَاهُ مَبْسُوطَتَانِ يُنفِقُ كَيْفَ يَشَآءُ ۚ وَلَيَزِيدَنَّ كَثِيرًا مِّنْهُم مَّآ أُنزِلَ
إِلَيْكَ مِن رَّبِّكَ طُغْيَٰنًا وَكُفْرًا ۚ وَأَلْقَيْنَا بَيْنَهُمُ ٱلْعَدَٰوَةَ وَٱلْبَغْضَآءَ إِلَىٰ
يَوْمِ ٱلْقِيَٰمَةِ ۚ كُلَّمَآ أَوْقَدُوا۟ نَارًا لِّلْحَرْبِ أَطْفَأَهَا ٱللَّهُ ۚ وَيَسْعَوْنَ فِى
ٱلْأَرْضِ فَسَادًا ۚ وَٱللَّهُ لَا يُحِبُّ ٱلْمُفْسِدِينَ ﴿٦٤﴾

The Jews say, 'Allah's hand is tied up.' Tied up be their hands and cursed be they for what they say! Rather, His hands are wide open: He bestows as He wishes. Surely many of them will be increased by what has been sent to you from your Lord in rebellion and unfaith, and We have cast enmity and hatred amongst them until the Day of

[77] Quran, Sūrah al-Nisā' (4), Verse 46.

Resurrection. Every time they ignite the flames of war, Allah puts them out. They seek to cause corruption on the earth, and Allah does not like the agents of corruption.[78]

3. Malediction against the Polytheists

﴿وَيُعَذِّبَ ٱلْمُنَٰفِقِينَ وَٱلْمُنَٰفِقَٰتِ وَٱلْمُشْرِكِينَ وَٱلْمُشْرِكَٰتِ ٱلظَّآنِّينَ
بِٱللَّهِ ظَنَّ ٱلسَّوْءِ ۚ عَلَيْهِمْ دَآئِرَةُ ٱلسَّوْءِ ۖ وَغَضِبَ ٱللَّهُ عَلَيْهِمْ وَلَعَنَهُمْ
وَأَعَدَّ لَهُمْ جَهَنَّمَ ۖ وَسَآءَتْ مَصِيرًا ٦﴾

That He may punish the hypocrites, men and women, and the polytheists, men, and women, who entertain a bad opinion of Allah. For them shall be an adverse turn of fortune: Allah is wrathful with them, and He has cursed them, and prepared for them hell, and it is an evil destination.[79]

4. Malediction against Specific Individuals from among the People of the Book

4.1 Those who Disregarded the Sabbath

﴿قُلْ هَلْ أُنَبِّئُكُم بِشَرٍّ مِّن ذَٰلِكَ مَثُوبَةً عِندَ ٱللَّهِ ۚ مَن لَّعَنَهُ ٱللَّهُ
وَغَضِبَ عَلَيْهِ وَجَعَلَ مِنْهُمُ ٱلْقِرَدَةَ وَٱلْخَنَازِيرَ وَعَبَدَ ٱلطَّٰغُوتَ ۚ
أُو۟لَٰٓئِكَ شَرٌّ مَّكَانًا وَأَضَلُّ عَن سَوَآءِ ٱلسَّبِيلِ ٦٠﴾

[78] Quran, Sūrah al-Mā'idah (5), Verse 64.
[79] Ibid., Sūrah al-Fatḥ (48), Verse 6.

Say, 'Shall I inform you concerning something worse than that as a requital from Allah? Those whom Allah has cursed and with whom He is wrathful, and turned some of whom into apes and swine, and worshippers of the Rebel! Such are in a worse situation, and more astray from the right way.'[80]

4.2 Claimants that the hands of Allah ﷻ are "Tied"

﴿وَقَالَتِ ٱلْيَهُودُ يَدُ ٱللَّهِ مَغْلُولَةٌ ۚ غُلَّتْ أَيْدِيهِمْ وَلُعِنُوا۟ بِمَا قَالُوا۟ ۘ بَلْ
يَدَاهُ مَبْسُوطَتَانِ يُنفِقُ كَيْفَ يَشَآءُ ۚ وَلَيَزِيدَنَّ كَثِيرًا مِّنْهُم مَّآ أُنزِلَ
إِلَيْكَ مِن رَّبِّكَ طُغْيَـٰنًا وَكُفْرًا ۚ وَأَلْقَيْنَا بَيْنَهُمُ ٱلْعَدَٰوَةَ وَٱلْبَغْضَآءَ إِلَىٰ
يَوْمِ ٱلْقِيَـٰمَةِ ۚ كُلَّمَآ أَوْقَدُوا۟ نَارًا لِّلْحَرْبِ أَطْفَأَهَا ٱللَّهُ ۚ وَيَسْعَوْنَ فِى
ٱلْأَرْضِ فَسَادًا ۚ وَٱللَّهُ لَا يُحِبُّ ٱلْمُفْسِدِينَ ﴿٦٤﴾﴾

The Jews say, 'Allah's hand is tied up.' Tied up be their hands and cursed be they for what they say! Rather, His hands are wide open: He bestows as He wishes. Surely many of them will be increased by what has been sent to you from your Lord in rebellion and unfaith, and We have cast enmity and hatred amongst them until the Day of Resurrection. Every time they ignite the flames of war, Allah puts them out. They seek to cause corruption on the earth, and Allah does not like the agents of corruption.[81]

---

[80] Quran, Sūrah al-Mā'idah (5), Verse 60.
[81] Ibid., Sūrah al-Mā'idah (5), Verse 64.

5. Malediction against Specific Individuals who claimed to be Muslims

5.1 The Hypocrites

﴿وَعَدَ ٱللَّهُ ٱلْمُنَٰفِقِينَ وَٱلْمُنَٰفِقَٰتِ وَٱلْكُفَّارَ نَارَ جَهَنَّمَ خَٰلِدِينَ فِيهَاۚ
هِىَ حَسْبُهُمْۚ وَلَعَنَهُمُ ٱللَّهُۖ وَلَهُمْ عَذَابٌ مُّقِيمٌ ٦٨﴾

Allah has promised the hypocrites, men, and women, and the faithless, the Fire of hell, to remain in it [forever]. That suffices them. Allah has cursed them, and there is a lasting punishment for them.[82]

﴿وَيُعَذِّبَ ٱلْمُنَٰفِقِينَ وَٱلْمُنَٰفِقَٰتِ وَٱلْمُشْرِكِينَ وَٱلْمُشْرِكَٰتِ ٱلظَّآنِّينَ
بِٱللَّهِ ظَنَّ ٱلسَّوْءِۚ عَلَيْهِمْ دَآئِرَةُ ٱلسَّوْءِۖ وَغَضِبَ ٱللَّهُ عَلَيْهِمْ وَلَعَنَهُمْ
وَأَعَدَّ لَهُمْ جَهَنَّمَۖ وَسَآءَتْ مَصِيرًا ٦﴾

That He may punish the hypocrites, men and women, and the polytheists, men, and women, who entertain a bad opinion of Allah. For them shall be an adverse turn of fortune: Allah is wrathful with them, and He has cursed them, and prepared for them hell, and it is an evil destination.[83]

﴿لَّئِن لَّمْ يَنتَهِ ٱلْمُنَٰفِقُونَ وَٱلَّذِينَ فِى قُلُوبِهِم مَّرَضٌ وَٱلْمُرْجِفُونَ فِى
ٱلْمَدِينَةِ لَنُغْرِيَنَّكَ بِهِمْ ثُمَّ لَا يُجَاوِرُونَكَ فِيهَآ إِلَّا قَلِيلًا ٦٠
مَّلْعُونِينَۖ أَيْنَمَا ثُقِفُوٓاْ أُخِذُواْ وَقُتِّلُواْ تَقْتِيلًا ٦١﴾

---

[82] Quran, Sūrah al-Tawbah (9), Verse 68.
[83] Ibid., Sūrah al-Fatḥ (48), Verse 6.

> If the hypocrites do not relinquish and [also] those in whose hearts is a sickness, and the rumormongers in the city [do not give up], We will surely urge you [to act] against them, then they will not be your neighbours in it except for a little [while]. Accursed, they will be seized wherever they are confronted and slain violently.[84]

5.2 The "Cursed Tree" in the Quran

﴿وَإِذْ قُلْنَا لَكَ إِنَّ رَبَّكَ أَحَاطَ بِٱلنَّاسِ ۚ وَمَا جَعَلْنَا ٱلرُّءْيَا ٱلَّتِىٓ أَرَيْنَٰكَ إِلَّا فِتْنَةً لِّلنَّاسِ وَٱلشَّجَرَةَ ٱلْمَلْعُونَةَ فِى ٱلْقُرْءَانِ ۚ وَنُخَوِّفُهُمْ فَمَا يَزِيدُهُمْ إِلَّا طُغْيَٰنًا كَبِيرًا ٦٠﴾

> When We said to you, 'Indeed your Lord comprehends all humanity,' We did not appoint the vision that We showed you except as a test for the people and the cursed tree in the Quran. We deter them, but it only increases them in great rebellion.[85]

As has been affirmed in the authentic aḥādīth of the Prophet ﷺ narrated by all Muslims (Sunni and Shīʿa) the meaning of the 'cursed tree' as spoken about in the Noble Quran is the Umayyad dynasty. To better appreciate this understanding, please reflect upon the follow traditions narrated by the Sunni and Shīʿa.

In his exegesis under the verse mentioned above, Ibn Jarīr al-Ṭabarī narrates the following statement from Sahl ibn Saʿd: "The Messenger of Allah saw the clan of so-and-so (the Umayyad dynasty) in a dream depicted as monkeys climbing up and down on his pulpit *(mimbar)*. This brought immense grief to the Prophet such that from that point up until his death, he was

[84] Quran, Sūrah al-Aḥzāb (33), verses 60 & 61.
[85] Ibid., Sūrah al-Isrā' (17), Verse 60.

never seen smiling and it was the following verse which Allah revealed to him regarding what he saw in his dream: "...We did not make the vision that We showed you (during the Ascension) but as a trial for humankind to mend their ways..."[86]

In his exegesis of the Noble Quran in regards to the verse mentioned above, Al-Qurṭubī relates from Sahl ibn Saʿd that: "This vision (dream) which the Messenger of Allah saw in which he witnessed monkeys ascending and descending from his pulpit *(mimbar)* is in regards to the Umayyad dynasty after which he became extremely depressed and from that day forward until his death, he was never seen to laugh and the verse [under review] was revealed to confirm to the Prophet that after him, they would take over the reins of governance of the Islamic community and that Allah, the Most High would refer to this as a test and tribulation which would be imposed upon the people."

It has been narrated from Yūnis ibn ʿAbd al-Raḥmān ibn al-Ashal that he asked one of the Imams in regards to the statement of Allah: "...We did not make the vision that We showed you (during the Ascension) but as a trial for humankind to mend their ways..." and the Imam replied: "The Messenger of Allah saw a dream in which certain members of the Umayyad dynasty were ascending and descending from his pulpit and anytime one ascended, they would prevent people from traversing the path of Allah.

The Messenger of Allah saw the humiliation [of Islam and his community] in his dream and with a feeling of great anguish and distress, he woke up from his sleep. It has been narrated that the number of individuals which the Prophet saw in his dream were twelve – all belonging to the Umayyad family and their dynasty.

---

[86] This portion of the verse states:

...وَمَا جَعَلْنَا ٱلرُّءْيَا ٱلَّتِيٓ أَرَيْنَٰكَ إِلَّا فِتْنَةً لِّلنَّاسِ...

It was at this point that the Angel Jibrā'īl descended and conveyed this verse of the Quran to the Prophet.

It has been narrated by Imam Muḥammad ibn ʿAlī al-Bāqir ﷺ that he said: "The verse of the Quran: "...We did not make the vision that We showed you (during the night journey) but as a trial for humankind to mend their ways..." was in reference to the masses who would be confused (in that era) and that the "cursed tree" mentioned in the Quran was a reference to the Umayyad dynasty."

6. Malediction against People – Muslims and non-Muslims

6.1 Those who Cause Grief to Allah ﷻ and his Messenger ﷺ

﴿إِنَّ ٱلَّذِينَ يُؤْذُونَ ٱللَّهَ وَرَسُولَهُۥ لَعَنَهُمُ ٱللَّهُ فِى ٱلدُّنْيَا وَٱلْـَٔاخِرَةِ وَأَعَدَّ لَهُمْ عَذَابًا مُّهِينًا ﴿٥٧﴾﴾

Indeed, those who torment Allah, and His Apostle are cursed by Allah in this world and in the Hereafter, and He has prepared for them a humiliating punishment.[87]

6.1.1 Hurting Imam ʿAlī ﷺ is like hurting the Prophet ﷺ

In a tradition from Abī Yaʿlī from Saʿd it has been narrated that: "I was sitting with two people in the *masjid,* and we were complaining about ʿAlī, and [in the vicinity] was the Messenger of Allah who, upon hearing what we were saying, became enraged and this was evident from the change in his face. We

[87] Quran, Sūrah al-Aḥzāb (33), Verse 57.

sought refuge in Allah from the anger of the Prophet and at that point the Prophet said to us: 'What problem do you have with me? [Know that] whoever has hurt or offended ʿAlī has insulted me.'"

In his *Mustadrak*, al-Ḥākim narrates from ʿUmru ibn Sās Aslamī (one of the companions present in *Ḥudaybiyyah*) that he said: "I had gone with ʿAlī to Yemen (on an expedition). While on the trip, he did something to me that upset me. When we returned [to Medina], I openly raised my objections against what he had done to me in the *masjid*, and my statements made their way to the ears of the Messenger of Allah. The next morning, I went to the Masjid and saw the Messenger of Allah sitting among a group of his companions and when he laid his eyes on me, I saw anger in him. I sat down and he continued to look at me with anger in his eyes and then he said to me: 'O ʿUmrū! I swear by Allah that you have indeed insulted me.' I said to him, 'I seek refuge in Allah that I should ever do something to offend you O' Messenger of Allah!' He replied, 'Indeed whoever offends ʿAlī has indeed offended and insulted me.'"

After mentioning this, Ḥākim goes on to say: "This *ḥadīth* has a sound chain of transmission, however those two (al-Bukhārī and al-Muslim) have not mentioned this in their books. In addition, al-Dhahabī has said that this tradition is sound."

Ibn Ḥabbān, in his *Ṣaḥīḥ* has narrated this in his book of collections.

Al-Haythamī, in his book, *Majmaʿ al-Zawāid*, has narrated [the same] traditions as quoted above and then states, "[Imam] Aḥmad and al-Ṭabarānī have also narrated the same traditions in a shortened format and al-Bazzār has narrated the same in an even shorter format and according to [Imam] Aḥmad, the chain of narrators is trustworthy."

It has been narrated from ʿUmrū ibn Shaʾn that: "The Prophet said, 'Indeed you have upset me.' I said to him, 'O Messenger of

Allah! I do not like to hurt you.' To this he replied, 'Whoever hurts ʿAlī has hurt me.'"

6.1.2 Hurting Fāṭima az-Zahrāʾ ﷺ is like hurting the Prophet ﷺ

Prophet Muḥammad ﷺ has made the following statements:

إِنَّمَا فَاطِمَةَ بَضْعَةٌ مِنِّي يُؤْذِينِي مَا آذَاهَا

> Indeed, Fāṭima is a part of me – that which hurts me hurts her.

فَاطِمَةَ بَضْعَةٌ مِنِّي يُرْبِينِي مَا أَرْبَاهَا وَ يُؤْذِينِي مَا آذَاهَا

> Indeed, Fāṭima is a part of me – that which distresses me, also distresses her and that which hurts me, hurts her.

إِنَّمَا فَاطِمَةَ بَضْعَةٌ مِنِّي يُؤْذِينِي مَا آذَاهَا وَ يَنْصُبَنِي مَا أَنْصَبَهَا

> Indeed, Fāṭima is a part of me – that which hurts me, hurts her and that which grieves me also grieves her.

6.2 Those who Lie

﴿فَمَنْ حَآجَّكَ فِيهِ مِنۢ بَعْدِ مَا جَآءَكَ مِنَ ٱلْعِلْمِ فَقُلْ تَعَالَوْا۟ نَدْعُ أَبْنَآءَنَا وَأَبْنَآءَكُمْ وَنِسَآءَنَا وَنِسَآءَكُمْ وَأَنفُسَنَا وَأَنفُسَكُمْ ثُمَّ نَبْتَهِلْ فَنَجْعَل لَّعْنَتَ ٱللَّهِ عَلَى ٱلْكَٰذِبِينَ ﴿٦١﴾﴾

> Should anyone argue with you concerning him, after the knowledge that has come to you, say, 'Come! Let us call our sons and your sons, our women and your women, our

souls, and your souls, then let us pray earnestly and call down Allah's curse upon the liars.'[88]

6.3 Those who Kill Innocent People

﴿وَمَن يَقْتُلْ مُؤْمِنًا مُّتَعَمِّدًا فَجَزَآؤُهُۥ جَهَنَّمُ خَٰلِدًا فِيهَا وَغَضِبَ
ٱللَّهُ عَلَيْهِ وَلَعَنَهُۥ وَأَعَدَّ لَهُۥ عَذَابًا عَظِيمًا﴿٩٣﴾﴾

Should anyone kill a believer intentionally, his requital shall be hell, to remain in it [forever]; Allah shall be wrathful at him and curse him and He shall prepare for him a great punishment.[89]

6.4 The Oppressors and Despots

﴿يَوْمَ لَا يَنفَعُ ٱلظَّٰلِمِينَ مَعْذِرَتُهُمْ ۖ وَلَهُمُ ٱللَّعْنَةُ وَلَهُمْ سُوٓءُ ٱلدَّارِ﴿٥٢﴾﴾

The day when the excuses of the wrongdoers will not benefit them, and the curse will lie on them, and for them will be the ills of the [ultimate] abode.[90]

﴿وَنَادَىٰٓ أَصْحَٰبُ ٱلْجَنَّةِ أَصْحَٰبَ ٱلنَّارِ أَن قَدْ وَجَدْنَا مَا وَعَدَنَا
رَبُّنَا حَقًّا فَهَلْ وَجَدتُّم مَّا وَعَدَ رَبُّكُمْ حَقًّا ۖ قَالُوا۟ نَعَمْ ۚ فَأَذَّنَ مُؤَذِّنٌۢ
بَيْنَهُمْ أَن لَّعْنَةُ ٱللَّهِ عَلَى ٱلظَّٰلِمِينَ﴿٤٤﴾﴾

The inhabitants of paradise will call out to the inmates of the Fire, 'We found what our Lord promised us to be true; did you find what your Lord promised you to be true?'

---

88 Quran, Sūrah Ale 'Imrān (3), Verse 61.
89 Ibid., Sūrah al-Nisā' (4), Verse 93.
90 Ibid., Sūrah al-Ghāfir (40), Verse 52.

'Yes,' they will say. Then a caller will announce in their midst, 'May Allah's curse be upon the wrongdoers!'[91]

﴿وَمَنْ أَظْلَمُ مِمَّنِ ٱفْتَرَىٰ عَلَى ٱللَّهِ كَذِبًا ۚ أُو۟لَٰٓئِكَ يُعْرَضُونَ عَلَىٰ رَبِّهِمْ وَيَقُولُ ٱلْأَشْهَٰدُ هَٰٓؤُلَآءِ ٱلَّذِينَ كَذَبُوا۟ عَلَىٰ رَبِّهِمْ ۚ أَلَا لَعْنَةُ ٱللَّهِ عَلَى ٱلظَّٰلِمِينَ ﴿١٨﴾﴾

And who is a greater wrongdoer than him who fabricates a lie against Allah? They shall be presented before their Lord, and the witnesses will say, 'It is these who lied against their Lord.' Look! The curse of Allah is upon the wrongdoers.[92]

6.5 Those who Falsely Accuse Women of Adultery

﴿وَٱلْخَٰمِسَةُ أَنَّ لَعْنَتَ ٱللَّهِ عَلَيْهِ إِن كَانَ مِنَ ٱلْكَٰذِبِينَ ﴿٧﴾﴾

And a fifth [oath] that Allah's wrath shall be upon him if he were lying.[93]

﴿إِنَّ ٱلَّذِينَ يَرْمُونَ ٱلْمُحْصَنَٰتِ ٱلْغَٰفِلَٰتِ ٱلْمُؤْمِنَٰتِ لُعِنُوا۟ فِى ٱلدُّنْيَا وَٱلْءَاخِرَةِ وَلَهُمْ عَذَابٌ عَظِيمٌ ﴿٢٣﴾﴾

Indeed, those who accuse honourable and unwary faithful women shall be cursed in this world and in the Hereafter, and there shall be a great punishment for them.[94]

---

[91] Quran, Sūrah al-Aʿrāf (7), Verse 44.
[92] Ibid., Sūrah al-Hūd (11), Verse 18.
[93] Ibid., Sūrah al-Nūr (24), Verse 7.
[94] Ibid., Verse 23.

6.6 Those who Break their Oaths Made to Allah ﷻ

﴿وَٱلَّذِينَ يَنقُضُونَ عَهۡدَ ٱللَّهِ مِنۢ بَعۡدِ مِيثَٰقِهِۦ وَيَقۡطَعُونَ مَآ أَمَرَ
ٱللَّهُ بِهِۦٓ أَن يُوصَلَ وَيُفۡسِدُونَ فِي ٱلۡأَرۡضِ أُوْلَٰٓئِكَ لَهُمُ ٱللَّعۡنَةُ وَلَهُمۡ
سُوٓءُ ٱلدَّارِ ٢٥﴾

But as for those who break Allah's compact after having pledged it solemnly, and sever what Allah has commanded to be joined, and cause corruption in the earth —it is such on whom the curse will lie, and for them will be the ills of the [ultimate] abode.[95]

6.7 Those who Attribute Falsehood Against Allah ﷻ

﴿وَمَنۡ أَظۡلَمُ مِمَّنِ ٱفۡتَرَىٰ عَلَى ٱللَّهِ كَذِبًاۚ أُوْلَٰٓئِكَ يُعۡرَضُونَ عَلَىٰ رَبِّهِمۡ
وَيَقُولُ ٱلۡأَشۡهَٰدُ هَٰٓؤُلَآءِ ٱلَّذِينَ كَذَبُواْ عَلَىٰ رَبِّهِمۡۚ أَلَا لَعۡنَةُ ٱللَّهِ عَلَى
ٱلظَّٰلِمِينَ ١٨﴾

And who is a greater wrongdoer than him who fabricates a lie against Allah? They shall be presented before their Lord, and the witnesses will say, 'It is these who lied against their Lord.' Look! The curse of Allah is upon the wrongdoers.[96]

---

[95] Quran, Sūrah al-Raʿd (13), Verse 25.
[96] Ibid., Sūrah Hūd (11), Verse 18.

6.8 Those who Hide the Truths of Allah ﷻ

﴿فَبَدَّلَ ٱلَّذِينَ ظَلَمُوا۟ قَوْلًا غَيْرَ ٱلَّذِى قِيلَ لَهُمْ فَأَنزَلْنَا عَلَى ٱلَّذِينَ
ظَلَمُوا۟ رِجْزًا مِّنَ ٱلسَّمَآءِ بِمَا كَانُوا۟ يَفْسُقُونَ ٥٩﴾

Indeed, those who conceal what We have sent down of manifest proofs and guidance, after We have clarified it in the Book for mankind,—they shall be cursed by Allah and cursed by the cursers.[97]

6.9 Those who Consider the Jews to be Better than the Muslims

﴿أَلَمْ تَرَ إِلَى ٱلَّذِينَ أُوتُوا۟ نَصِيبًا مِّنَ ٱلْكِتَٰبِ يُؤْمِنُونَ بِٱلْجِبْتِ
وَٱلطَّٰغُوتِ وَيَقُولُونَ لِلَّذِينَ كَفَرُوا۟ هَٰٓؤُلَآءِ أَهْدَىٰ مِنَ ٱلَّذِينَ ءَامَنُوا۟
سَبِيلًا ٥١ أُو۟لَٰٓئِكَ ٱلَّذِينَ لَعَنَهُمُ ٱللَّهُ ۖ وَمَن يَلْعَنِ ٱللَّهُ فَلَن تَجِدَ لَهُۥ
نَصِيرًا ٥٢﴾

Have you not regarded those who were given a share of the Book believing in idols and the Rebel and saying of the pagans: 'These are better guided on the way than the faithful'? They are the ones whom Allah has cursed, and whom Allah curses, you will never find any helper for him.[98]

[97] Quran, Sūrah al-Baqarah (2), Verse 59.
[98] Ibid., Sūrah al-Nisā' (4), verses 51 & 52.

6.10 Those who Create Corruption on the Earth and Break Family Ties

﴿فَهَلْ عَسَيْتُمْ إِن تَوَلَّيْتُمْ أَن تُفْسِدُوا۟ فِى ٱلْأَرْضِ وَتُقَطِّعُوٓا۟ أَرْحَامَكُمْ ﴿٢٢﴾ أُو۟لَٰٓئِكَ ٱلَّذِينَ لَعَنَهُمُ ٱللَّهُ فَأَصَمَّهُمْ وَأَعْمَىٰٓ أَبْصَٰرَهُمْ ﴿٢٣﴾﴾

May it not be that if you were to wield authority you would cause corruption in the land and ill-treat your blood relations? They are the ones whom Allah has cursed, so He made them deaf, and blinded their sight.[99]

[99] Quran, Sūrah Muḥammad (47), verses 22 & 23.

Sources

Al-Bidāyah wa al-Nihāyah by Abū al-Fidā' Ismā'īl ibn 'Umar ibn Kathīr al-Qarashī

Al-Kāfī by Shaykh al-Kulaynī

Musnad by Aḥmad ibn Ḥanbal

Al-Nihāyah fil Gharīb al-Ḥadīth wa al-Athar by Abū as-Sa'ādāt al-Mubārak ibn Muḥammad al-Jazarī

Biḥār al-Anwār by Muḥammad Bāqir al-Majlisī

Dalīl al-Murshidīn ilā'l Ḥaqqil Yaqīn by Ja'far Subḥānī

Jāmī' al-Bayān fī Ta'wīl al-Quran by Abū Ja'far al-Ṭabarī

Mufradāt Alfādh al-Quran by Rāghib Iṣfhānī

Mustadrak 'alā al-Ṣaḥīḥḥayn by Ḥākim al-Nishābūrī

Nahj al-Balāgha by Sayyid Raḍī

Rāhnumā-i Ḥaqīqah by Ja'far Subḥānī

Ṣaḥīḥ al-Bukhārī

Ṣaḥīḥ al-Muslim

Shī'a Shināsī wa Pāsukh be Shubuhāt by 'Alī Aṣghar Riḍwānī

Sunan Abī Dāwūd by Abū Dāwūd Sulaymān ibn al-Ash'ath al-Sijistānī

Tafsīr al-Kabīr by Fakhr al-Dīn al-Rāzī

Tārikh al-Umam wa al-Mulūk by Abū Ja'far Muḥammad ibn Jarīr al-Ṭabarī

The Noble Quran

Wasā'īl ash-Shī'a by Shaykh Ḥurr 'Āmilī

Other Publications Available[1]

1. *A Land Most Goodly: The Story of Yemen in the Quran and in the Times of Prophet Muḥammad and Imam ʿAlī ibn Abī Ṭālib* by Jaffer Ladak
2. *A Star Amongst the Stars: The life and times of the great companion: Jabir ibn Abdullah al-Ansari* by Jaffer Ladak
3. *Alif, Baa, Taa of Kerbala* by Saleem Bhimji, and Arifa Hudda
4. *Arbāʿīn of Imam Ḥusayn* compiled and translated by Saleem Bhimji
5. *Contentious Issues in Islamic History - ʿUmar ibn al-Khaṭṭāb* written by Saʿīd Dāwarī and translated by Saleem Bhimji
6. *Deficient? A Review of Sermon 80 from Nahj al-Balāgha* by Āyatullāh al-ʿUẓmā Shaykh Nāṣir Makārim Shīrāzī and translated by Saleem Bhimji
7. *Exegesis of the 29th Juz of the Quran - a translation of Tafsīr Namuneh* by Āyatullāh al-ʿUẓmā Shaykh Nāṣir Makārim Shīrāzī and translated by Saleem Bhimji

---

[1] The following is a list of all original writings and translations from the Islamic Publishing House. As many of these titles are out of stock, we are re-releasing all our works via Print-on-Demand through Amazon.

Search for the title that you are looking for via Amazon on one of their international platforms, including: Australia, Canada, France, Germany, Italy, Japan, UK, USA, Netherlands, and Spain.

If you cannot find any of the above titles on Amazon, feel free to email us at *iph@iph.ca.*

8. *Foundations of Islamic Unity* - a translation of *Al-Fuṣūl Al-Muhimmah fī Taʾlīf al-Ummah* by ʿAbd al-Ḥusayn Sharaf al-Dīn al-Mūsawī al-ʿĀmilī and translated by Batool Ispahany
9. *Fountain of Paradise - Fāṭima az-Zahrāʾ in the Noble Quran* by Āyatullāh al-ʿUẓmā Shaykh Nāṣir Makārim Shīrāzī, compiled and translated by Saleem Bhimji
10. *God and god of Science* by Syed Hasan Raza Jafri
11. *House of Sorrows* by Shaykh ʿAbbās al-Qummī and translated by Aejaz Ali Turab Husayn Husayni
12. *Inspirational Insights* by Mohammed Khaku
13. *Islam and Religious Pluralism* by Āyatullāh Shaykh Murtaḍā Muṭahharī and translated by Sayyid Sulayman Ali Hasan
14. *Journey to Eternity - A Handbook of Supplications for the Soul* compiled and translated by Saleem Bhimji and Arifa Hudda
15. *Living The Quran Through The Living Quran: Sūrah al-Najm - A Translation of Tafsīr Nūr* by Shaykh Muḥsin Qarāʾatī and translated by Saleem Bhimji
16. *Living The Quran Through The Living Quran: Sūrah Qāf - A Translation of Tafsīr Nūr* by Shaykh Muḥsin Qarāʾatī and translated by Saleem Bhimji
17. *Love and Hate for Allah's Sake* by Mujtabā Ṣabūrī translated by Saleem Bhimji
18. *Love for the Family* compiled and translated by Yasin T. Al-Jibouri, Saleem Bhimji, and others
19. *Moral Management* by ʿAbbās Rahīmī and translated by Saleem Bhimji
20. *Morals of the Masumeen* by Arifa Hudda
21. *Prayers of the Final Prophet - A collection of supplications of Prophet Muḥammad* by ʿAllāmah Sayyid Muḥammad Ḥusayn Ṭabāʾṭabāʾī and translated by Tahir Ridha-Jaffer

22. *Prospering Through a Cost of Living Crisis* by Jaffer Ladak
23. *Ramaḍān Reflections* compiled by A Group of Muslim Scholars and translated by Saleem Bhimji
24. *Ṣalāt al-Āyāt* by Saleem Bhimji
25. *Ṣalāt al-Ghufaylah: Salvation through Patience & Perseverance* written by Saleem Bhimji
26. *Secrets of the Ḥajj* by Āyatullāh al-ʿUẓmā Shaykh Ḥusayn Mazāherī and translated by Saleem Bhimji
27. *Sunan an-Nabī* by ʿAllāmah Sayyid Muḥammad Ḥusayn Ṭabā'ṭabā'ī and translated by Tahir Ridha-Jaffer
28. *Tears from Heaven's Flowers: An Anthology of English Poetry about the Ahlulbayt* by Abrahim al-Zubeidi
29. *The Firmest Armament: Commentary on Āyatul Kursī (The Verse of the Throne)* by Sayyid Naṣrullāh Burujerdī and translated by Saleem Bhimji
30. *The Last Luminary and Ways to Delve into the Light* by Sayyid Muḥammad Riḍā Ḥusaynī Muṭlaq and translated by Saleem Bhimji
31. *The Muslim Legal Will Booklet* by Saleem Bhimji
32. *The Pure Life* by Āyatullāh al-ʿUẓmā as-Sayyid Muḥammad Taqī al-Modarresī and translated by Jaffer Ladak with commentary by Dr. Zainali Panjwani and Jaffer Ladak
33. *The Third Testimony: Imam ʿAlī in the Adhān* compiled and translated by Saleem Bhimji
34. *The Torch of Perpetual Guidance - A Brief Commentary on Ziyārat al-ʿĀshūrā'* by ʿAbbās ʿAzīzī and translated by Saleem Bhimji
35. *The Tragedy of Karbalā' by Imam ʿAlī ibn al-Ḥusayn as-Sajjād and translated by ʿAbdul-Zahrā' ʿAbdul-Ḥussain*

36. *Weapon of the Believer* by ʿAllāmah Muḥammad Bāqir Majlisī and translated by Saleem Bhimji

In addition to these titles which are currently available, look for our series of booklets featuring the commentary of the Noble Quran entitled *Living the Quran Through The Living Quran - A Translation of Tafsīr Nūr* of Shaykh Muḥsin Qarā'atī. This series of booklets will be available exclusively from Amazon.

www.ingramcontent.com/pod-product-compliance
Lightning Source LLC
Chambersburg PA
CBHW061732040426
42453CB00026B/975
9781927930441